Praise for *Hip & Sage* and Lisa Haneberg

"*Hip & Sage* is a must-have book for mature professionals who want to remain relevant and leave a legacy. Lisa's wit and wisdom are in full force as she offers examples and strategies to help us be hip and sage."
—MARSHALL GOLDSMITH, THE NYT AND WSJ #1 BEST-SELLING AUTHOR OF *WHAT GOT YOU THERE WON'T GET YOU THERE*

"If it wasn't for the amazing Elmore Leonard, this book should have been titled…*BE COOL*. *Hip & Sage* will give you all the confidence and skill needed to be the coolest of the cool in every business situation…not only will you become fluent in the Zeitgeist but you'll master cross-generational relationships in a way never dreamed possible."
—VINCE THOMPSON, AUTHOR OF *IGNITED: MANAGERS! LIGHT UP YOUR COMPANY AND CAREER FOR MORE POWER, MORE PURPOSE AND MORE SUCCESS*

"Experienced business leaders today need to connect in new ways online, engage people differently and learn new technologies. You can either shake your head in frustration or learn from Lisa exactly how to master the paradox of the new open online world and the traditional depth of personal connections and experience."
—MICHAEL KANAZAWA, CO-AUTHOR, *BIG IDEAS TO BIG RESULTS* AND CEO, DISSERO PARTNERS

"*Hip & Sage is very timely as many Boomers are looking to work past their normal retirement age and be valued in the marketplace.*"
—GURURAJA YELLAPUR, FOUNDER OF BOOMER411

Hip & Sage

Hip
& Sage

Staying Smart, Cool and Competitive in the Workplace

LISA HANEBERG

D|B

Davies-Black
an imprint of Nicholas Brealey Publishing
Boston • London

First published by Davies-Black, an imprint of Nicholas Brealey Publishing, in 2009.

20 Park Plaza, Suite 1115A	3–5 Spafield Street, Clerkenwell
Boston, MA 02116, USA	London, EC1R 4QB, UK
Tel: + 617-523-3801	Tel: +44-(0)-207-239-0360
Fax: + 617-523-3708	Fax: +44-(0)-207-239-0370

www.nicholasbrealey.com

Special discounts on bulk quantities of Davies-Black books are available to corporations, professional associations, and other organizations. For details, contact us at 888-273-2539.

Printed in the United States of America

13 12 11 10 09   10 9 8 7 6 5 4 3 2 1

ISBN: 978-0-89106-245-5

Library of Congress Cataloging-in-Publication Data

Haneberg, Lisa.
    Hip & sage : staying smart, cool and competitive in the workplace / Lisa Haneberg.
        p. cm.
    Includes bibliographical references and index.
        ISBN 978-0-89106-245-5 (pbk.)
        1. Intergenerational relations. 2. Intergenerational communication. 3. Work.
    I. Title.

HM726.H34 2009
305.2—dc22
200803992

Contents

Preface

I fear the morning I wake up irrelevant. It will happen, I know, but I am determined to put off that day for as long as I can. How about you? This book is written for the amazing and mature Baby Boomers who want to apply their experience and knowledge while excelling in the new world of business.

My friend Leigh asked me what started my interest in and journey toward becoming (and staying) hip and sage. Here is the story I shared with her:

I attended a *Fast Company* magazine readers network meeting in late 2004. The small group of about eight professionals struck me as being smart, curious, and interesting. I sat near Lori, a sales consultant, and Curt, a "passion catalyst," who were talking about their **blogs (weblogs).**[1] I wondered what a blog was. I heard them use words and phrases such as **permalinks, trackbacks,** and **Carnival of the Capitalists** as they discussed strategies for building blog readership.

As I listened, I began to panic because I had no idea what they were talking about. Lori and Curt were not techies—people for whom computer technology forms the center of their universe—they were business consultants. After about thirty minutes, I mustered the courage to reveal my ignorance and ask

---

1. To help with the sometimes dizzying jargon of hipness, at the back of the book is "A Glossary of Hip." The first time a term included in the glossary is used in the text, it will appear in bold type.

them about these terms. They were generous and spent the rest of the evening—about ninety minutes—mentoring me about the world of blogging. My mind bubbled over as ideas about how I might use blogging to build my consulting practice percolated. I needed to get caught up. After I got home from the *Fast Company* event, I created my first blog and named it Management Craft (still going strong today at www.managementcraft.com). Within the first week, I figured out what permalinks were and how to use them to link to posts on other blogs. Within two weeks, I was using trackbacks to notify other bloggers when I linked to their posts. Within three months, I hosted the Carnival of the Capitalists—a weekly event that lists and links to the best business blog posts from the previous week and that is hosted each week by a different blogger.

I am a red caboose Baby Boomer, born in the final Boomer year: 1964. I blog, **podcast,** network online, **text message,** deliver **webinars,** and have a video posted on **YouTube.** When young readers e-mail me or comment on my blog and tell me I am hip or cool, or that my post was awesome, I giggle with delight. My **RSS feeds** have thousands of daily subscribers, and my blogs get more than a thousand hits from Google per day. If you don't understand what all this means, you need not worry—you soon will.

Leigh says I am hip and sage, and I love hearing that, but hip is a moving target and we need to stay aware of and engaged in what's happening now—how people are communicating and doing business this month. We don't need to become super-geeks or learn to write **HTML code,** but we do need to know how to find and reach out to our business partners, clients, peers, and employees. In the fall of 2004, I discovered blogging. Today, I have additional interests and questions. *I'm not **twittering**—should I be twittering?* One thing I know for sure—I have a need to feel relevant and to be able to communicate in ways that are both contemporary and effective.

Podcasts, **iPods,** YouTube, **Flickr,** live chats, texting, blogging, **plogging,** and **vlogging.** New technologies are changing the way we meet, talk, and learn. Multitasking, **webcasts, unconferences,** and **streaming video** are common tools for the younger generations. The workplace is changing in other ways too; there is greater interest in flextime, telecommuting, freelancing, and virtual and cross-functional international teams.

It's nothing new that things are changing. Since the Industrial Revolution, business practices have lasted less than a geologic second. The phrase "flavor of the month" migrated from conversation about ice cream to discussion about the latest buzzwords and management fads. We Baby Boomers have seen many changes, but what's different now is that we are the ones who need to keep up. We are the ones others might perceive as being rigid, averse to change, slow, or stuck in the past. When you have decades of experience weighing you down, change can be daunting and draining.

Baby Boomers who learn to embrace workplace changes will find they can contribute to their organizations and businesses in new and better ways. Millions will start new businesses, but only those who can compete in the new marketplace will be successful. Knowing about **search engine optimization (SEO)** is as fundamental to today's businesses as being able to balance a checkbook.

Being hip and sage is an approach to business and career and is not achieved by creating a blog or learning how to podcast. While it is important that we be able to communicate using the methods our employees and customers prefer, being hip is much more than this. Our hipness determines how well we connect and collaborate with younger generations. Hip and sage professionals will have a competitive advantage over their contemporaries who do not get hip. They challenge younger generations and raise the level of business for all the players in their markets.

Hip & Sage has been fun to write, although I have taken a few risks with obsolescence. Some of the examples I have shared about new technologies will have become out-of-date before ink hits this page. Who knows? We might not be twittering at all by the time you read these words. This is fine, because it is the principles of **hipness** and **sageness** that are most important and useful.

The book has several short chapters and a few long ones. The short chapters are conversation starters. They are appetizers to whet your appetite for the information included in the long chapters. The short chapters tell stories, and the longer chapters explain and illustrate the definitions of sageness and hipness. As noted earlier, I have included a glossary of terms in the "Resources" section—the first time a term included in the glossary is used in the text, it will appear in **bold** type. (There have been several instances already!)

I interviewed a number of hip and sage professionals and have sprinkled several quotes from our conversations throughout the book. The "Resources" section offers additional information about topics that support but are tangential to the main creative arc that holds together *Hip & Sage*. In addition to the glossary, you will find a primer on the generations and recommended books and other information sources.

I enjoyed digging into the meaning of sageness and how we season and polish our lives so that we can be powerful mentors and role models for later generations. Hip and sage professionals are wonderful and varied creatures, brimming with useful knowledge and thirsting for continued learning. They are blazing new trails for ways to leave a business legacy—with their correctional shoes, titanium hips, and 160GB video iPods hooked to their belts.

Meet Hip & Sage

I was talking on the phone with Dan Pink about his latest book, *The Adventures of Johnny Bunko,*[1] when the conversation turned to the topic of Tony Bennett.

> **Lisa:** I don't know if you watch the *Sunday Morning* show on CBS, but several weeks ago, they did a profile of musician k.d. lang. They asked her about an album she had done with Tony Bennett back in 2002. The interview then cut to a prerecorded piece with Tony Bennett where he was asked about his work with k.d. lang and how they met. Bennett said that he was backstage at a Grammy show and he saw k.d. lang, walked up to her, extended his arm, and said, "I'm Tony Bennett, and someday I'd love to sing with you." I found this story amazing. First of all, backstage at the Grammys, Tony Bennett does not need to tell people that he is Tony Bennett.

> **Dan:** Yeah, yeah, yeah.

> **Lisa:** Can you imagine what it must have been like to be k.d. lang having Tony Bennett walk up and say this? Well, if you import that example into the professional

---

1. You can find Dan Pink's Web site at www.danpink.com, and I have listed two of his books in the "References and Recommended Reading" section in the back of the book.

world, what would happen if you had a forty-five-, fifty-five-, or sixty-year-old middle or senior manager—someone who's been around forever—walk up to one of the new engineering recruits and say, "Hey, Johnny, I've heard a lot about you, and I just want you to know that I'm really eager to learn from you, and I'd love to work with you on a project one day."

Dan: Yeah, that's great.

Lisa: So I think there can be a shift in mentality about how we approach working with younger professionals. Instead of a mind-set of earning the gold watch, being entitled, and needing to figure out how to relate to the strange and lazy young people for a few more years, what if we became fans of new talent—like Tony Bennett with k.d. lang? There's humbleness, humility, and something that comes with that mind-set. What's possible with this strategic shift in thinking? What's possible when we are eager and curious about what younger folks bring to the table and how they bring it to the table? Here's another way this could look—a fifty-something professional walks up to a thirty-something and says, "I love what you are sharing in your presentations, but I've got to tell you, I don't understand it all. Would you be willing to teach me about the new technologies and methods you advocate using?"

Dan: What you're talking about is an awesome strategy. And I think that the Tony Bennett story is terrific. You should call that "the Tony Bennett Strategy" or something like that.

Let's take a fresh look at partnership with those strange and mysterious beings we call the younger generations. After seeing the k.d. lang–Tony Bennett feature on the *Sunday Morning* show, I shared the story with dozens of people and wrote about it on my blog. What blows me away—the reason I have retold this story again and again—is that it clearly illustrates the power of a humble hip and sage mind-set. If you remember nothing else from this book, I would like you to remember this little story about Tony Bennett and k.d. lang.

Do you see Bennett's aproach in play at your workplace? Chances are, you more likely see polite but less engaging exchanges, like this imaginary alternative conversation between k.d. lang and Tony Bennett:

> k.d. lang bumps into Tony Bennett.
>
> She apologizes. "Mr. Bennett, so sorry."
>
> He is gracious. "No problem."
>
> "I loved the song you sang tonight; it's one of my favorites," she tells Bennett.
>
> "Thanks, that's very kind. I liked yours, too, kiddo."
>
> Uncomfortable, k.d. lang extends her hand. They shake and move on.

There's nothing wrong with this alternative outcome except that it would not have been magical—it would not have been the catalyst that led to a Grammy-winning collaboration and lifelong collegial relationship.[2] In a 2001 NPR interview lang

---

2. Tony Bennett and k.d. lang toured together in 2001. Their CD, *A Wonderful World,* won a Grammy Award.

said this about their collaboration: "I think there's some sort of innate understanding between Tony and I. In terms of the texture and intonation of our voices, I think there's a natural blend there and, certainly in spirit, there's a definite marriage there."[3]

I invite you to take on this powerful mind-set. Recognize and appreciate talent, wherever it may be. Anyone can be a fan of anyone. Anyone can collaborate. This mind-set comes from being comfortable in one's skin—but not cocky. Tony Bennett, with the help of his two sons, Danny and Dae, reinvented his career after tough times that began in the late 1960s and lasted until 1979, when he almost died of a cocaine overdose.[4] Bennett has reinvented himself as a singer and also as a painter and sculptor.[5]

I don't think you can change and remain relevant without doing a deep internal assessment of your thinking patterns, the ways in which you're behaving, how you are using your time, and how you are managing your work.
EFFENUS HENDERSON

---

3. Listen to Tony Bennett and k.d. lang on their NPR interview here: www.npr.org/templates/story/story.php?storyId=851987.

4. Being a crooner was decidedly unhip throughout most of the seventies. As the Beatles surged in popularity, crooners fell out of favor. Tony Bennett's record label, Columbia, suggested that he record more contemporary rock songs. His 1969 attempt, *Tony Bennett Sings the Great Hits of Today!* was unsuccessful. Bennett and Columbia Records parted ways. In the seventies, Tony Bennett started his own record label and recorded two albums under this label (Improv) with jazz pianist Bill Evans before the label went out of business in 1977. He developed a cocaine addiction, nearly went broke, and performed only in Las Vegas. The IRS tried to seize Bennett's L.A. home to pay for back taxes. Learn more about Tony Bennett's tough times and triumphant return to success here: www.biography.com/search/article.do?id=9926699.

5. See Tony Bennett's paintings here: www.tonybennett.com.

Would you like to reinvent your career? Would you like to experience a professional renaissance and feel reengaged in your work? Try putting Tony Bennett's approach to work for you. Here are a few examples of what it looks like in action:

- You walk up to a younger worker and introduce yourself, showing an interest in that worker's contribution.

- You tell a younger colleague what you admire about his or her work.

- You seek out projects so that you can work with younger colleagues.

- You let younger colleagues know that you admire their work and ask them to join your project team. Better yet, you ask one of them to lead the project team.

- With no particular project in mind, you let a younger colleague know that you would like to work together.

- At the end of a meeting, you tell a younger colleague that he or she did an amazing job.

- You ask younger colleagues for advice and guidance.

Try using the Tony Bennett approach this week. Practice with your kids or grandkids. Notice how you feel and observe their reactions. After a couple of times, I think you will get hooked. Being hip feels wonderful and allows your sageness to come out more fully. Imagine what's possible when you "Tony Bennett" in the workplace, and in your community.

For Tony Bennett, the k.d. lang conversation was just the beginning. He honed his hipness and became a popular performer all over again. After working with k.d. lang, Tony Bennett went on to produce a CD called *Duets,* where he paired up with folks like Bono from U2, Sting, country star Tim McGraw, and Latin American singer Juanes. His duet with pop star Christina Aguilera earned Bennett another Grammy nomination. And in true hip and sage form, he provides **link love** to all these performers' Web sites from his own site.[6] In the messages section of Bennett's site, a young fan posted a link to a YouTube video of a duet between Tony Bennett and the Backstreet Boys. They sang a Bing Crosby song. How delicious. Let's mix it up at work.

I have opened this book with the story about Tony Bennett because it sets the stage for the chapters that follow. I hope that this story has inspired you—and piqued your interest in learning more about how to be both hip and sage.

---

6. Tony Bennett's music Web site can be found here: www.tonybennett.net.

Sage

Sageness

Many people reserve the word *sage* for describing the select few people they believe possess profound wisdom. Philosophers and scientists such as Socrates, Confucius, Aristotle, Da Vinci, and Einstein often top the list of sages. While it is valuable and appropriate to honor select individuals who make significant and visible contributions to humanity, we should also recognize and appreciate the sageness that is within ourselves and those around us. The qualities that make us sages are what I call our *sageness*. I invite you to expand your notions about sageness.

> *We are happier in many ways when we are old than when we were young. The young sow wild oats. The old grow sage.*
> WINSTON CHURCHILL (1874–1965)

What we call things—the names and labels we use—is important. Our perceptions are shaped by the dialogue we use to describe what's happening in our world. Our reality is created in conversations. Here's an example. If I see a round wooden pedestal that is twenty-four inches high and twelve inches in diameter, I might sit on it and call this thing a stool. It is a stool to me and this is my reality. Imagine that a few minutes later, two five-year-old girls come upon the wooden pedestal and decide that it is a table that would be perfect to use for their tea party. Their reality is that it is a table because this is what they have named it and how they use it. Is it a stool or a table? Who is right? Both and neither. This is a simple example, but the same dynamic plays out in our everyday lives.

How does your reality change when you refer to yourself as a sage? Do you sit up a bit straighter? Think a bit deeper? Sigh a knowing sigh? Name yourself a sage and you become one. You are sage, and the knowledge you have gained is priceless. Here is my definition of sageness:

> **Sageness:** Our natural strengths and characteristics, goals and priorities, and experiences—manifested as skills, drive, judgment, and knowledge—that have been honed, carved, seasoned, and polished through the years. Our sageness is unique; it may or may not be visible to others or in use contributing to the world.

Our sageness determines how we will interact with the world. As we mature, learn, and gain experience, our approach focuses and deepens—we become more of what is at our core. The three parts of this definition of sageness represent who we are (inputs), how we refine who we are (processing), and what comes from these refinement processes (results). Figure 1 provides a graphical representation of sageness.

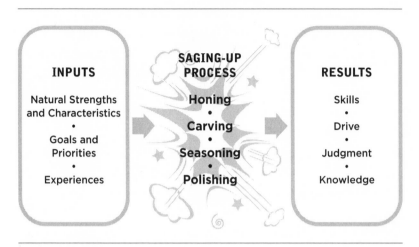

FIGURE 1 **SAGENESS**

INPUTS

Let's break down this definition further, starting with the first part—who we are, or the inputs. The three input elements are natural strengths and characteristics, goals and priorities, and experiences.

NATURAL STRENGTHS AND CHARACTERISTICS

Our natural strengths and characteristics form the foundation from which our sageness manifests—they are capabilities that give us energy and at which we naturally excel. We might need cultivation or education to build strengths—even the most gifted musicians take lessons and practice. Marcus Buckingham, author of several best-selling books, including *Now, Discover*

Your Strengths (coauthored by Donald Clifton), suggests that we fashion and arrange our lives to better explore and build our strengths.[1] Working with the Gallup research organization, Buckingham's company created the Strengths Finder, which is an assessment of one's natural strengths.[2] Examples of strengths include *achiever, competitor, developer,* and *learner.* You are probably aware of many of your strengths but not all. We can discover them at any time in life, and they tend to endure because they are natural, or comfortable, for us. Someone who has an amazing knack for selling was likely a good salesperson in grade school and will still be selling something after moving into a retirement community.

Our characteristics include our natural behavioral tendencies. If you have ever taken a behavioral assessment such as the *Myers-Briggs Type Indicator*® (MBTI®) instrument, DiSC, Social Styles, or Activity Vector Analysis, you have received feedback about your natural tendencies.[3] Our characteristics form an overall expression of our style or our natural reactions and behaviors. They determine how we come across to others, react under pressure, and approach our work. Examples of characteristics include *direct, assertive, reserved, gregarious, methodical, analytical, persuasive, driven, emotive, rhythmic, serious, expedi-*

---

1. You can find Marcus Buckingham's Web site here: www.marcusbuckingham.com. I did a podcast with Marcus Buckingham, which was a very interesting experience. You can find the podcast here: www.lisahaneberg.com/podcasts-and-webcasts.

2. If you buy *Now, Discover Your Strengths,* you will find a code inside that allows you to take the Strengths Finder Assessment. It is well worth it to buy the book and take the assessment. You can find out more information about the Strengths Finder assessment here: www.strengthsfinder.com.

3. Here is the link to find the MBTI assessment: www.mbticomplete.com. I have used this assessment for team building, and it is a great way to encourage conversation about natural styles and tendencies. My MBTI type is INTP, which has been described as "The Thinker." Hmmm . . .

tious, wary, and *friendly.* These characteristics are what enable our close friends and colleagues to predict how we will react and what types of situations will cause us pleasure or stress. As we sage up, our characteristics shape and develop, although they generally don't change a lot. A highly assertive person might become slightly less assertive but will not likely become passive.

GOALS AND PRIORITIES

Goals and priorities form the filter through which our sageness manifests. Our goals and priorities shape our sageness because they determine the directions we take our lives and how we choose to live. Goals are targets, and priorities are an expression of which targets are most important. Unlike strengths and characteristics, goals and priorities may change many times—sometimes dramatically—throughout our lives.

Goals become a filter for our sageness because they shape how we define success and how we approach opportunities, challenges, and options. For example, if entrepreneurialism and business development are important to you, and if you want to own and manage your own company (or do so more effectively), your sageness will have an entrepreneurial bent. You will seek learning and experiences that improve your awareness and skills for business development and you will talk more about business development. Your goals and priorities show up in the other two parts of the sageness model because they affect the daily choices you make.

If you endeavor to spend more time working on environmental education, you will apply your strengths toward environmental projects and education and engage others involved with the green movement. Your judgments and decisions will be informed and affected by this goal and its relative priority in your life. You are more likely to seek and take action in ways that reinforce your interest in environmental education.

EXPERIENCES

Intelligence comes from the practical actions and practices of our daily experiences—including things we learn from research and obsevation and by application. We learn and unlearn many things. We enjoy victories and suffer failures and along the way we build up a playbook for how things work. Experiences last forever and are like deposits into a savings account. You might need to use experiences, and they might just become a part of your overall intellectual assets. The types of experiences you have will shape your sageness.

Experiences define our worldliness—the breadth and depth and diversity of our data.[4] It used to be that worldliness came primarily from traveling—from seeing and learning firsthand about different cultures, countries, states, and ways of life. Technology now enables us to become more worldly by taking in communication from new cable channels, the Internet, and travel shows. Actual travel is still a wonderful way to broaden your perspectives, but it's no longer the only way.

Here is why our experiences are important when we consider sageness. Our experiences are the inputs that are most closely affected by time—by aging. Experience is often what makes the difference between achieving a success or suffering a setback. Two leaders who share similar strengths, characteristics,

---

4. In the early 1990s, I was certified by the Walter V. Clark Company to interpret the Activity Vector Analysis behavioral assessment. One aspect of the assessment measured a person's worldliness—the breadth of his or her experiences. Interestingly, worldliness was positively correlated with sound decision making and maturity.

goals, and priorities, but who have very different professional experiences, will differ in judgment, knowledge, and actions.

Many larger companies accelerate the experience-gathering process by providing leaders with rotating assignments, more training, and diverse projects. This approach works, and it creates a more worldly management team. Most of us gain experience through job changes, geographical moves, higher education, promotions and job moves, and regular attention to news programs and books.

In business, experiences add up to provide professionals with something called *business acumen*—knowledge of how the business works and its key drivers and measures for success. But a word of caution and a plug for the second half of the book— business acumen has an expiration date. Experiences are not a panacea for professionals seeking greater success because many things change—including how we conduct business, market our products and services, get work done, and measure business success.

So while experience is an element of sageness defined by our aging, it also has a shorter shelf life than other elements, and this is the reason you want to be both sage and hip. Some experiences have a very long shelf life—like the fundamentals we learn about human relations. This is why, seven decades after it was first published, Dale Carnegie's *How to Win Friends and Influence People* (1990) is still one of the best books available about human relations.[5] Other business challenges, like how to grow the target market for your products, how to create customer loyalty, how to motivate younger employees, or how to measure

---

5. I cannot stress my recommendation of this book enough. *How to Win Friends and Influence People* offers clear and forceful advice about how to build authentic relationships.

manufacturing effectiveness, will call for leaders with up-to-date experiences in these areas.

THE PROCESS OF SAGING UP

As inputs, our natural strengths and characteristics, goals and priorities, and experiences come together to form a basis of who we are at work and as leaders in our communities and families. As we age, we better understand what's at our core (strengths and characteristics) and continuously build and shape our goals, priorities, and experiences. These three elements get processed in the middle portion of the sageness model—a combined set of refinements that determine how we sage up. The four elements within the saging-up portion of the sageness model are honing, carving, seasoning, and polishing.

HONING

I love the word *hone* because it is a great way to describe how we choose things. To hone means to make something sharper, better focused, or more efficient. It comes from the Old English word *han,* which means stone, and it was first used to describe the process of sharpening a razor on a whetstone. To hone is to sharpen something for better use. We hone skills. We hone beliefs and judgments.

Training programs, apprenticeships, craft associations, and career paths are all designed to help professionals hone their skills and abilities. Some will hone more quickly or effectively than others, but honing is always a process that takes some time. More complex skills—managing people, for instance—take longer to hone. This is why even the most brilliant college students often struggle when placed in management positions right after graduation.

CARVING

Carving is one of the most fascinating and useful elements of the saging-up process. Carving is the act of taking material away in order to produce a better product or service. When we carve, we cut, shape, and etch, and we alter the appearance and size and shape of things. I talked with Dick Richards—author of *Is Your Genius at Work?* and other books—about the usefulness of carving in our lives.[6] He said:

> When I hear someone say the word carving, I think of Michelangelo, who was able to see the statue in the stone, and who saw his job as taking away everything that didn't serve the statue. He wasn't building a statue; he was removing what was in the way, and I see saging up as that kind of process. It's a process of looking at what it is about me that is in the way. Michelangelo called his genius intelleto—the ability to see what's there: to see the statue in the stone. Sageness involves removing the excess to improve clarity and vigor.

As we mature, we are better able to assess our daily lives and determine what's in the way of focusing on what matters most. Here are a few examples of what carving—as I am using the term here—looks like in action:

- Reducing a mile-long to-do list to the five most important tasks

---

6. You can find Dick Richards's blog, Come Gather Round, here: http://ongenius.com/blog/.

- Letting go of goals that are no longer a priority or will not make you happier or more fulfilled.

- Reducing the clutter in your life and workplace

- Saying no to opportunities that do not serve your goals and priorities

- Learning more about who you are and making choices consistent with your increased self-awareness

Imagine a beautiful statue stuck in a block of marble. Each chip of the carver's chisel reveals a bit more about the shape and the true nature of what's underneath. When we carve, we play the part of the artist whittling at the elements of our work, home, and leisure lives to fashion them into the right shape for us. In *Repacking Your Bags,* authors Richard Leider and David Shapiro use the metaphor of packing for a trip in a way similar to how carving is described here. They too stress the value in letting go of—or unpacking—things and habits that no longer enhance our lives. They write, "at every moment, in every situation, we are free to choose a simpler expression of our being. We always have the potential to unpack, lighten our loads, and repack" (Leider and Shapiro, 2002, p. 7).[7] At work, the strength, ability, and willingness to unpack and repack are enormously useful—imagine the outdated projects, obsolete processes, annoying tasks, useless traditions, and wasteful inefficiencies that could benefit from being unpacked and replaced by something better.

---

7. You can find Richard Leider's Web site here: www.inventurecoaching.com/. If the notion of repacking your bags is appealing, you will find several other books along these lines listed on the Web site. I reviewed another of Leider and Shapiro's books, *Claiming Your Place at the Fire,* which might be of interest to hip and sage professionals. You can find my review here: http://managementcraft.typepad.com/management_craft/2004/10/claiming_your _p.html.

SEASONING

When we season something, we add to it in tiny ways that make a big difference. Seasoning allows the natural assets of the product, service, or situation to come through in ways that are more pleasing, lively, or exciting. When we season foods while cooking, we add flavor, spice, and pizzazz.

Small additions can make a big difference, and we learn this as we sage up. A seasoned response in a meeting will add just the right amount of emphasis and emotiveness to the discussion. The seasoned approach will leave prospective clients feeling they are in good hands. Seasoning can be translated as *savvy, confident, engaging, brilliant, wise, unflappable,* or *magnetic,* just to name a few examples.

Seasoning adds a bit of magic to a dish. What separates the best chefs from the mediocre is often how they use spices and essences to bring out natural flavors. In woodworking, wood is seasoned to withstand the environmental elements (heat, rain, snow) in which it will be placed. Humid environments would require the wood to be seasoned quite differently than for desert climes. This is also true for business situations. We adjust the seasoning to fit the needs of the situation. Seasoned leaders—because they are able to bring in a little magic—enable people and processes to do their best work. Sage leaders tweak their style, delivery, actions, and decisions to improve communication, acceptance, and results. Knowing how to season your approach comes with time, observation, and practice. Training programs and college classes do not teach seasoning.

POLISHING

Polishing makes a surface smooth—we buff away the tiny roughnesses and we improve the object's feel. As we sage up, we polish our core skills, creating a more confident look and feel. Polishing can be editing an important e-mail for the fourth time, practicing a presentation, or making any of the tiny changes that suggest themselves after we've done similar tasks again and again.

What's the difference between seasoning and polishing? When we season, we add flavor and appeal. When we polish, we remove just a bit more to make our message or process clearer and more elegant. In writing, we polish when we remove needless words and revise to clarify our message.

Two leaders in a staff meeting can have access to the same facts and possess similar basic skills, but the one who is better able to apply polish will come across better. A couple of years ago, I heard author and über blogger Guy Kawasaki speak to a group of about three hundred business professionals.[8] He was funny, witty, and wise, and his presentation looked great and moved at an exciting pace. During the Q&A segment of the presentation, someone asked Guy how he prepared for speeches. Guy said that he practiced each presentation a minimum of forty times. He used a PowerPoint presentation with very few words, and his main points were powerful and provocative—there was no waste or excess in what we heard or saw. During the forty practice run-throughs, Guy applied polish to his messages and techniques.

The saging-up process is where we improve how we experience life. We hone, carve, season, and polish. Hone, carve, season, and polish. Hone, carve, season, and polish. Again and

---

8. Guy Kawasaki is a dynamic and interesting professional and I think he is old enough that he would also qualify as hip and sage. You can find Guy's blog, How to Change the World, here: http://blog.guykawasaki.com/. In 2004, I reviewed Guy's book *Art of the Start* on Management Craft. Read that here: http://managementcraft.typepad.com/management_craft/2004/11/guy_kawasakis_c.html.

again, the process continues. We become clearer about what's important and can point our lives in the optimal direction with vigor.

RESULTS

The third part of the sageness model is results. Through processing, our inputs (natural strengths and characteristics, goals and priorities, and experiences) are manifested as skills, drive, judgment, knowledge, and action. These results are what people see and experience from us. Skills, drive, judgment, and knowledge are what you have to offer in abundance. Let's dig deeper into each of these ingredients.

SKILLS

A skill is an ability to do something well. As we mature, we learn more skills and we become more skilled at the tasks on which we focus. I have played golf with my father approximately once a year for the past twenty years. In between the golf games with my dad, I do not pick up the golf clubs. I do not read about golf, and I don't watch it on the television. I have learned the basic skills of the game, but have not become skilled at any of them (except mulligans) because I do not practice. In golf, they talk about *muscle memory,* meaning the way repeatedly practicing a golf swing creates a path for the swing to follow again and again.

Unlike golf, management is something I have practiced for decades. My skills for managing have been honed, carved, seasoned, and polished, and this process will continue until I die or stop managing. I have muscle memory for how to manage. As we learn and develop our skills we build pathways, shortcuts, and databanks. We can do certain things quickly and well because our muscle memory allows us to perform skills with flow and efficiency. At work, our sageness shows up in our skills. Our experience is manifested as talent—an ability to get the work done with great acumen.

Relying on skills has a downside: skills become obsolete. As we mature, we become skilled at a large number of things, and some of these skills may not remain useful. Our mental pathways for how to get things done can fail to serve today's goals. When too many skills are no longer needed or valued, we risk becoming irrelevant. Many seemingly outdated skills can be used to bridge the gap between how work used to be done and how it ought to be done in the future.

For example, consider the skill of project management. Today, a lot of technology tools allow project leaders and teams to track and manage the flow of work within a project. Twenty years ago, we managed projects using handwritten spreadsheets and regular team meetings. Today's technologies for managing projects replace the handwritten spreadsheets but they might not replace the value achieved from face-to-face updates. Hip and sage leaders, who have experienced the value of relationship building within project teams, can tap into their background to ensure that technology does not become the source of the only tools used to manage the project. Hip and sage project managers also need to learn the new technology—but I will address this later in the book.

DRIVE

Drive is another word for motivation, defining what we are drawn to. When assessing drive, we need to evaluate the aspects of life and work that naturally draw us in and the reasons behind our choices. Drive and success are intertwined because our definitions of success are affected by our motivations. If we are driven to make money, we will define success in terms of wealth building. If we are driven to give back to the community, we will feel more successful if we improve the community. If we are motivated by status, we will see promotions and executive perks as the trappings of success.

As we sage up, we clarify and refine our motivations. This is a natural process that occurs because we learn what matters— what makes us happy—and what goals we ought to discard. We are driven by fewer goals but each means more—our drive is focused on the few goals that we feel are most important.

Drive is a result in the sageness model because it is something that comes out of honing, carving, seasoning, and polishing, and because it is visible. You may think that your motivations are internal and therefore unknown, but that is not the case. Although drive is internal, it is also easy to see based on the choices we make and how we respond to feedback and inquiries. In the workplace, our motivation is manifested daily. If people believe our drive runs counter to what is in the best interests of the company, it might be called a *personal agenda*. Some people are drawn to change, others to stability. After working with us for a couple months, people will learn—through our behaviors and choices—how we define success.

JUDGMENT

Judgment is our ability to make good decisions and sensible conclusions. Our judgment improves as we try and fail, try and succeed, and as we hone our perception of the characteristics of a good decision. Sound judgment is one of the more visible aspects of our sageness and should be a focus of the mentoring we provide to younger professionals. Education and worldliness improve judgment, but trial and error as well as reflection— which happen only over time—do more to inform our judgments. Judgment helps moderate knee-jerk reactions provoked by ego, fear, competitiveness, self-aggrandizement, envy, or glory.

Leaders with sound judgment make better decisions. In *The Right Decision Every Time,* author Luda Kopeikina studied the dynamics of decisions and why some leaders make better decisions than their less effective peers.[9] Luda spoke to more than a hundred CEOs from companies of various sizes and industries. She found differences between mature leaders (in terms of both years and experiences) and those with less seasoning and polishing. She found that mature leaders had more mental control and were focused and calm even when they had major meetings or urgent issues to resolve later in the day. Luda also found that sage leaders evaluated their decisions, learned from them, and were overall more reflective than younger leaders. She defines what she calls the clarity state:

> *The key to reaching clarity is the ability to focus your physical, mental, and emotional resources at will on a certain issue. With such focus, you can identify the right choice faster, more easily, and with greater certainty and internal alignment. It is a practice that can be acquired.* (2005, p. 11)

The clarity state is an observable mental, physical, and emotional coherence that focuses our inner resources so we can make better decisions—and we tend to get better at this as we mature—as we sage up.

---

9. Find out more about this book and Luda Kopeikina here: www.ludakopeikina.com/.

KNOWLEDGE

Knowledge is tough to define. It starts with skills and experiences, but having a skill does not give someone knowledge. Knowledge is what we acquire when we are able to apply context and judgment to our skills and experiences. Drawing from my earlier example about my pitiful golf game, I have some skills for how to play golf. I would not say that I have developed knowledge of golf. Contextual elements in golf include the rules, traditions, and current trends. If I practiced more, I would develop better judgment about club choices and swing strategies. If I applied skills, context, and judgment to golf, I would build knowledge. Could someone have knowledge of golf without ever having played the game? While you could learn context elements of golf and, through observation, develop judgment about golf, unless you also practiced golf, your knowledge of it would be strictly academic. For our purposes here and as it relates to sageness, I define *knowledge* as what comes from the application of skills, context, and judgment. Knowledge is what is in your human databank, put into a usable context.

The sageness comes from where the knife of my creativity meets the wood of life experiences.
OLIVER PICHER

SAGENESS

That's sageness—the inputs, the processing, and the results. Our sageness begins developing when we are young and gets stronger, clearer, and more useful over time. The way in which we sage up and the pace at which we become honed, carved, seasoned, and polished people is individual and unique— although there are some recognizable signs of sageness. As we sage up, we learn that the things we know we don't know, and the ones we don't know we don't know, vastly outnumber and outweigh the things we know. This famous quote from Socrates reinforces this point well: "The only true wisdom is in knowing you know nothing." In addition, sageness facilitates a better understanding for how we fit in the world and how we can best make a positive contribution. Our goals begin to shift from ego driven to motivated by altruism and service. With sageness comes humbleness because we know we don't know and we define success in terms of contribution. Here is another thought from Dick Richards:

> *If I had twenty people lined up in front of me, and I was interviewing them with the idea to predict which one would be most sage, I would look for the person with little ego. I would look for humility. I would look for someone who knows it's not about them anymore.*

Socrates said, "Wisdom begins in wonder." Later in the book I focus on how hipness can help improve sageness by jacking up our abilities to learn from and relate to younger professionals. Sageness is the source of our exuberance, and hipness is the vehicle for continued development and relevancy.

In the next chapter, I explore how to discover and grow our sageness.

Cultivating Our Sageness

I hope my model of sageness has resonated with you. I also hope that it has you thinking about how you manifest your sageness at work and in play. You might also be wondering how you can cultivate or strengthen your sageness. As I did the research for this book, the people I would characterize as hip and sage shared a deep love for lifelong learning that affected their daily choices about work habits and hobbies. Their reality was that learning was fun and a privilege, and their mantra was *I love to learn!* Imagine how their lives would have looked and felt different had their mantra instead been *I can't understand all this new stuff.* If the latter statement were their mantra, they would have avoided new experiences and clung to the processes and practices that felt comfortable and easy to perform. They would have learned less, sought out fewer new experiences, and engaged with a narrower group of people.

Remember, what we call things matters. Learning is a catalytic process that facilitates and cultivates sageness—it deepens and sharpens as we become more experienced and worldly. The saging-up process is like any other craft—our sageness develops over time—and it cannot be rushed. Like fine wine, cheese, and whiskey, we slowly get better with age. And while we cannot leapfrog the natural process, we can do some things to speed up and deepen our saging up. This chapter offers ways you can cultivate your sageness.

Meet Hip and Sage: An Enigma Named Ralph

As he walked on the hollow hardwood stage, Ralph's worn and scarred plain brown cowboy boots boomed and echoed. He looked, spoke, and even moved a bit like John Wayne. A hero with big flaws. Several hundred middle and senior-level managers from a midwestern Fortune 500 company—many of them wearing navy blue suits and red-striped power ties—looked up at him.[1] I was one of the middle managers. The company had hired Ralph to kick off a yearly management conference held in its worldwide headquarters city. Ralph's job was to get us started, motivate us to think differently, and reinforce a number of points that our company's senior leaders had apparently failed to communicate successfully. Ralph projected a colorful PowerPoint presentation onto the stage wall, which was a bigger deal back in 1997 than it would be today. Ralph shared two-by-two models, charts with boxes and arrows, and pithy one-liners framed around a well-told story about how he had turned his company around.

---

1. The red power tie was made famous by President Ronald Reagan in the 1980s. According to www.askmen.com, the power tie has diagonal lines and may also be called a regimental tie. "Every politician has one, and so should every businessman."

Ralph started the meeting off, said what our leaders could not in ways they had not, and then kept going—an enigmatic combination of strength and softness, confidence and humility, with popular business jargon wrapped and re-phrased in his gritty style. The blue suits shifted in their chairs and took a few notes, but their eyes rarely strayed from where Ralph stood on the vast wooden stage.

As employees of a conservative and often unexciting large company over a hundred years old, we weren't really ready for Ralph. What took us by surprise, why our eyes were glued up toward and on him, was Ralph's willingness to be vulnerable, to show us that he was fallible and share his success story—a considerable financial achievement—with humility.

Ralph said that *he* had been the problem with his busi-ness, that *he* was the one who had needed to change, and told us—not sugarcoating the less flattering details—*who* he had had to become. He asked questions that probably pro-voked private "oh, shit" moments for half the blue suits in the room. I believe all great leaders learn lessons along the way, but Ralph surprised us that day with his story of how he learned to lead by being a better follower. It was on this morning that I first began distinguishing and thinking about what sageness could look like in business. Ralph used his own version of Tony Bennett's approach and reinvented his company and his career as its CEO.

My leadership team ended up working with Ralph sev-eral times over the next year. Once we flew up to Ralph's company and toured his facilities. I was struck by how Ralph and his employees—most much younger—communicated and connected. At the plant, the culture oozed mutual re-spect and cross-position collaboration. Ralph employed sev-eral of the methods I review in this chapter, and he credited them with helping him move from near curmudgeon to hip and sage leader within a few years.

I've identified seven practices to cultivate sageness. Each of these practices is built on the belief that lifelong learning is the key to staying relevant at our workplaces and in our communities. If we take on the mantra *I love learning,* doing so will serve us well. Each practice addresses one of the three parts of sageness: input, the saging-up process, and results. Together these practices provide a comprehensive program for cultivating sageness. Here are the seven practices:

The 7 Practices of Sageness

- Increasing your self-awareness (input)
- Setting better goals (saging up)
- Broadening your perspectives (saging up)
- Doing one great thing each day (results)
- Undoing and unpacking (results)
- Volunteering to be a mentor (results)
- Writing (results)

INCREASING YOUR SELF-AWARENESS

Here's a powerful belief that I suggest you take in and live by—*our strengths and weaknesses are known.* Sounds simple enough, doesn't it? People notice those who are charismatic, the ones who get defensive in meetings, and the ones with the habit of passing the buck. Unless you are a recluse working on top-secret projects that no one knows about, your strengths and weaknesses are on display. The reason that this belief is helpful is that once you believe that your strengths and weaknesses are already known, it makes sense to believe that openly discussing them has no downside. If I am a bad listener, people know this. I will incur no harm—and considerable benefit—if I share with my coworkers, even the younger ones, that I am working on becoming a better listener. People will not respect me any less for admitting what they already know—they are likely to respect me more for admitting it and saying I intend to do better. When we believe that our strengths and weaknesses are known, the mental garbage that often gets in the way of open conversations about growth and success evaporates.

Our strengths and weaknesses are known—by others. The question is, do we know? We don't want to be the last to know if we have a habit or trait that is driving people nuts or derailing their work. We don't want to be the last to know that we have an amazing talent that is going undeveloped and underutilized.

Do you know what your natural strengths are? In chapter 1, I shared a few resources that might help you assess strengths and behavioral tendencies (Marcus Buckingham's Strengths Finder and the *Myers-Briggs Type Indicator*® instrument). I like Marcus Buckingham's definition of a strength. He says that a strength is an activity that gives you energy and makes you feel strong. In other words, whether something is a strength or a weakness is related to how it makes you feel. Weaknesses, according to Buckingham, are activities that drain you and make you feel weak.

We have a greater potential to develop sageness in the area of our natural strengths, so it is helpful to have an awareness of our strengths. Another assessment I like is called Human

Dynamics.[2] The Human Dynamics styles are self-diagnosed without any check-in-the-box-type survey. You can read the book or attend a class and, after learning about the styles they measure, self-identify your natural preferences.

Sometimes, your strengths hit you over the head with a proverbial two-by-four and scream *look at me*. This happened to me recently at an author reading. I was attending a reading for an author who had been a guest on my podcast the previous week. After exchanging hellos, the author told me that he appreciated the way I did the podcast and that it seemed so natural to me, like it was my calling. I reflected on his comment later and for several days after the reading. The word *calling* kept seeping into my thoughts. He thought this was my calling? Had I ever considered that doing podcast interviews might be a calling for me? What is a calling? Gregg Levoy, author of *Callings*, wrote this about what happens when we train ourselves to listen to that which calls us:

> *Part of this discipline is being willing to contend with what we hear when we turn on our receivers. By being willing to receive, we, in a sense, will the calls to happen, to make themselves known.* (1998, p. 4)[3]

What's calling you? Whatever it is, it will be time well spent to explore the calls and determine if you should follow them. Our self-development time is best spent discovering and cultivating our strengths.

---

2. You can check out the Human Dynamics Web site here: www.humandynamics.com.

3. You can learn more about Gregg Levoy's work about callings by visiting his Web site: www.gregglevoy.com.

SETTING BETTER GOALS

As we get older, the quality of our goals matters more. We have less time to waste and we ought to be more right about which goals to chase after. Goals are our compass—they keep us going in a particular direction. I have worked with a lot of people who are held back by crummy or uninspiring goals. Here is a brief primer on how to select and define better goals.

Our goals should move us—inspire us—make the fine hairs on the backs of our necks tingle and stand up. Unfortunately, many goals fail to do more than remind us of what we have not yet accomplished. Here are some common reasons why many goals fall short:

- The goal is not really our goal—it's someone else's. I would expect that by the time we become hip and sage, we are no longer living our lives based on what other people think, but some of us still struggle with this.

- The goal doesn't define our contribution; it is too general or relates to what other people ought to do (for example: I want my granddaughter to get better grades).

- The goal is too broad or too narrow. If a goal is too broad, it will fail to help us focus on what's most important. If a goal is too narrow, it might not allow for wonderful and unexpected breakthroughs to happen.

- The goal is too unrealistic or not unrealistic enough. If a goal seems wholly doable, it is probably not big enough— not very inspiring. If a goal is completely unrealistic, it will lead to frustration and disappointment.

- The goal is too difficult to communicate.

Here are a few examples of goals that need refining:

- I want to save $300,000 more before I retire.

- I want to get promoted within six months.

- I want to get my degree before turning sixty.

- I want to climb Mt. Kilimanjaro.

- I want to exercise more.

CHARACTERISTICS OF GREAT GOALS

Great goals share the following characteristics.

Meaningful and inspiring. This is not the time to wimp out or get conservative—our sageness and our legacies are at stake! Achieving a goal takes work, so it should be something that we can get excited about and that will change our lives. Our goals must be worthy of extraordinary effort. We determine how we will live based on goals. Test: You'll know your goal is meaningful and inspiring when thinking about it makes you smile inside.

Applicable to you. This is an important distinction for the hip and sage because we might have a tendency to set goals for our friends, family, and coworkers. I worked with a mother who wanted her son to get better grades. This was not a good goal for her because it was not clear who should be taking action. A better way to express this goal would be this: "I want to provide the coaching, support, and ideas that will help my son willingly achieve excellent grades and do his best in school."

Something you want. Your goals should be something you want to achieve even if the work will be hard or uncomfortable or require life changes. Promotions and more money are rarely compelling enough on their own. Everyone wants more money! I know that many hip and sage workers are concerned about their retirement funds and this might be a compelling driver. But drivers are different from goals. Drivers help determine how much energy we pour into a task and for what reasons. Goals steer our decisions. Define your goals based on the contributions you want to make to your organization, business, or family.

Challenging but achievable. I think our goals should seem almost impossible and perhaps a bit crazy. Play full-out. Do you think Lance Armstrong's goals were conservative? Are the Google founders thinking small? No, of course not. Think big and set goals that scare you a bit.

On the other hand, some people create goals that are unrealistic or impossible and this is not good either. Going from GED to PhD in a year is unrealistic and would not be a good goal. Going from no business to a comfortable retirement in one year is unrealistic. Unrealistic goals will hinder our progress and deflate our energy and passion. Play big on the right playing field.

EXAMPLES OF GREAT GOALS

Here are a few good examples:

- I am an explorer at heart and I work for a company dedicated to enriching the spirit of outdoor exploration. I am surrounded by inspiration! Starting this quarter and growing each year, I want to plan and enjoy several short and at least one long journey of exploration that stretches my mind and body. I will begin with [one specific journey].

- I want to manage in such a way that I am able to create an environment where my employees can and want to do their best work. I want to leave a legacy by being a positive role model and inspiration for excellence every day.

- I've been wanting to get my master's degree for twenty years, but frankly, I could not get excited enough to make it happen. Most of the business degrees I looked at seemed boring, so I have decided to get my MFA (master of fine arts degree) and would like to begin this fall. My goal is to complete the program in two years, being open and coachable the whole way.

- I find the new technologies fascinating, and I have so much to learn. My mind spins with joy thinking about the possibilities! I want to create a business plan proposal, highlighting new technologies, that allows my company to build its product line and customer base.

Zowee! Imagine sharing those goals with a perfect stranger while waiting in line to buy tickets to see a Tony Bennett concert. You will change that person forever (and yourself, too)! Goals are how we define what success looks like—Ralph told us that setting better goals was one of the most important improvements he and his management team made. If you create better goals, you will have a better compass to help you steer your work and life. Sage professionals should cut through the list of so-so goals and zoom in on targets worthy of our time and attention.

BROADENING YOUR PERSPECTIVES

In 2007, I drove my motorcycle 9,400 miles through thirty-eight states. The trip took forty days. I was struck by how much I did not know about my own country! Many of my preconceived notions about places and the people in them were wrong, and it was a delight to experience the country in a whole new way. I have traveled to the Bering Sea, Mexico, New Zealand, Italy, Thailand, the United Kingdom, France, and many other places. Each trip has done double duty—vacation and learning experience.

I have been blogging since 2004 and I have over a hundred other blogs in my aggregator. Many of the bloggers live in other countries or work in industries unfamiliar to me. It is fascinating to read about the situations they face and the way they perceive the world. Blogs are particularly good at broadening perspectives because they are written in an informal voice and tend to contain more emotion, detail, and opinions than books or articles on the topic. I have found that my travels and my blog reading have helped me become a more worldly individual.

Ralph broadened his perspectives by collaborating—as a participant, not just as the CEO—more fully with his employees and customers. By building relationships he had not taken the time to cultivate before, he learned much about his own business. This leader-to-collaborator reinvention helped Ralph improve product quality and profitability and launch several new products.

I am using the word *worldly* to mean the breadth of our experiences and influences. Broad perspectives help us make better decisions and set more compelling life goals. Why? We have more information and context. New perspectives can also affect our motivations. I remember hearing a woman being interviewed on the *Oprah Winfrey Show* about her trip to rural Africa. After meeting the people and learning about their lives, she changed her career and started a nonprofit organization that raises money to build schools in rural Africa.

We can broaden our perspectives in many ways besides traveling—for example, by reading, participating in clubs, attending conferences, watching quality television programs, and working with diverse people (in terms of age, skill sets, profession, gender, national origin, and so on).

This practice—*broadening your perspectives*—is the easiest included in this chapter because all you need to do is learn and experience new things. It's possible to become a wee bit more worldly in just minutes a day. Even so, the comfort of familiar patterns can be a barrier to worldliness. If you live in the same place for a long time, hang around with the same small group of friends, read a narrow selection of books, watch a few favorite television programs, and work with the same small group of people on the job, you will struggle to broaden your perspectives and develop worldliness.

Shake things up a bit! If you can afford it, travel to new places and seek to meet people with whom you have little in common. You will learn a great deal and the experience will surely change you. If you cannot afford to travel, become an armchair traveler by reading great books about exotic places. Read blogs written by people in other states and countries (many are written in English, even if this is not the author's first language). Learn about different faiths, political systems, and food cultures. Study space exploration and the animal world. Rent one foreign film a month. If you generally read murder mysteries, slip in a book of essays every third book.

Join a new club. Take a class. Volunteer at the Humane Society or at the zoo.

Worldliness gives us strength and confidence and makes our sageness shine with polish. Our broad experiences season how we interpret the world in ways that will benefit many aspects of our lives.

DOING ONE GREAT THING EACH DAY

You have heard of the self-fulfilling prophecy and the Pygmalion effect, right? Both of these concepts theorize that expectations affect outcomes. If we have low expectations for ourselves, we are likely to get what we expect—low performance. If we have high expectations, performance will be higher. We rise to the level of expectations.

If you endeavor to do one great thing a day, you will accomplish more of what's most important. In the absence of establishing an intention to do one great thing, our expectations of ourselves often fall into the category of *work hard and do what you can.* The problem with the *do your best* expectation is that it is too vague and not inspiring.

It would be unrealistic to suggest spending time only on the work that is most important. We all have mile-long to-do lists filled with mundane tasks that need to get done. This is why I love the practice of doing one great thing each day. We can all do one great thing—even if it is a very small great thing.

> **Great thing:** A task that enables us to move closer to an important goal by making something new happen or removing a barrier to forward movement.

Your great thing could be a five-minute conversation or a four-hour planning session.

To determine your one great thing for today ask yourself the following question: *What's the one thing I could do today that would be the best use of my time?* Do that one thing! When we expect that we will do one great thing, we tune our choices to ensure that we deliver. As you get better at selecting and completing great tasks, you will find that you are doing more than one great thing each day. Here are a few more questions that will help you hone your ability to determine great things to do each day:

- Relative to all the things I could be doing, is this something that will have the greatest impact on my most important goals?

- Will this task improve results or effectiveness beyond what I am doing today?

- Will anyone notice if I don't do this?

- If I were thrust into an emergency today, and I could do only two other tasks, what would I do and would the other tasks on my task list still seem important?

Doing one great thing helps cultivate sageness because it focuses a portion of your daily energies on furthering your most important goals. Define success as using your time in ways that add the greatest value and impact.

UNDOING AND UNPACKING

In chapter 1, I shared a quote from *Repacking Your Bags* about how we tend to carry too much baggage around with us—real and metaphorical baggage. I love the notion of paring down distractions to experience life more fully. Most of us have too much stuff! Too many things going on. Too many limiting opinions. Too much extra weight. As we sage up, we learn what we should undo, not do, or leave behind.

We can build sageness by getting better at carving distractions away from our lives. Admittedly, this is the practice that I most need to follow myself. I have far too many things going on. I am working on projects that will not improve my happiness or help me achieve my most important goals. And I have surrounded myself with way too much stuff and my bags are about to burst at the seams—cars, condos, cats and dogs, books, handbags, expired vitamins, and bright plastic containers filled with years of excess things.

Because I cannot claim to be an expert with this practice, I will share with you the advice of authors Richard Leider and David Shapiro:

> We keep adding things and responsibilities until we get to the point we can't carry them anymore: It's the "Packing Principle." What then, is the solution? There are two parts to it: First decide how much you're really willing to carry. And second, decide what goes and what stays. (2002, p. 50)

Leider and Shapiro use the word *carry* in a broad sense—it could mean what we literally carry in our bags, briefcases, and bodies (our stuff) and also what we carry in terms of commitments, worries, and relationships. To assess what we are carrying and whether we should continue to carry it, we need to ask lots of questions about each aspect of our life and how well it helps us thrive and accomplish our goals. To do this you have to have some idea about where you want your life to head—in what directions you want to take your work and personal lives.

Have you made commitments that you now regret? Many of us are so nice that we would not think of pulling out of commitments. But think it through. What would happen if you undid a few things? Is there a way you can renegotiate a few commitments so that the outcome is a win-win for all involved? With some thought, you will often find an honorable way to undo commitments that you now know you should not have made in the first place (or can't keep up because conditions have changed).

When we align what we are carrying, in terms of life loads, we are better able to express our strengths and tap into what's most important. We are better able to use our sageness to help ourselves and others.

VOLUNTEERING TO BE A MENTOR

I attended a weeklong training program about fifteen years ago. The topic was leadership, but what most interested me was watching how the learning methods built into the program changed how we interacted with the material. The trainers used an approach called *each-teach* that went something like this: The instructor gave us a brief introduction to the material we were going to learn. He broke the class into groups of three or four people and gave each group a handout. We were to learn the material written up in the handout and then present a lesson for the rest of the class that would teach them the material. He gave us a total of thirty minutes to work as a team and fifteen minutes to present the material to the whole class.

Here is what I found fascinating. We listened and read differently because we knew we would have to teach the information to others. We read the handouts with focus and we deliberated about the topic as if we really cared about it. Since attending this training session, I have noticed this same dynamic play out again and again. We relate to our work and our hobbies in a much deeper way when we think we will be called on to teach others.

Mentoring, coaching, teaching, and facilitating are all excellent ways to learn and to engage with people and topics at a deeper level. Many of us feel a desire to give back—to share our sageness—and we should all seek ways to mentor others. You can initiate informal mentoring situations by inviting colleagues for a coffee chat. You can volunteer for formal mentoring programs at work or in your community.

Many people think that mentors are giving to others, but I think that mentoring is a wonderful way to learn and receive *from* others. We often learn more than do the people we mentor!

WRITING

I am admittedly biased in favor of this practice. I think that everyone should write on a regular basis for two reasons. First, I find that writing keeps me on my toes and helps me process my thoughts and freshen my opinions. The writing I have done on my blogs and in my books has required me to stay up-to-date on the topics that I write about. I love this! And the process of writing forces me to organize my information. Writing his book, for example, has tuned my understanding of my own sageness and helped me align my life so that I can continue to be hip and sage.

You don't have to write a book to benefit from writing (although I believe we all have at least one good book in us). I worked with one gentleman who wrote short essays, some just one page long, about the things he remembered about his life. He eventually did put the essays together into a book, by the way, which was a gift to his family that helped him reconnect with his life.

As we age, writing grows in importance and we have more to write about! I have worked with both of my parents (who each wrote a book of stories) and have taught writing courses for seniors, and I have seen the difference writing can make in our lives. The act of recording stories, experiences, and opinions makes the past and the present come to life. Writing is a very active practice.

Whether you write in a journal on a daily basis or write stories or essays, the practice of writing will help you understand and cultivate your sageness. Blogging is a great option too, because a blog is like a journal that others can read and comment about. If you are not currently a writer, you might enjoy taking a class. Most community colleges offer adult continuing education classes in writing for a small fee.

REGULAR PRACTICE

These seven practices are just a few of the ways we can continue to cultivate our sageness and align our lives to support our most important goals. As with any practice, being deliberate and performing regularly is more effective than being a weekend warrior with sporadic performance. This is because learning builds on the lessons that we have already learned. Lifelong learning practices help us stay engaged and give us the skills and knowledge we need to be sage and hip.

Hip

3

Hipness

I wrote a blog post about hipness on Management Craft in March 2007.[1] In the post I asked, Do we need to be hip? When I wrote the post, I had a particular definition of what it means to be hip in mind—one not very different from the definition I offer in this book. What surprised me was that a couple of people commented who had very different notions of what being hip meant. Wally said that hip is about style and fashion, not about management tools and techniques. Mark wrote that he thought being hip implied that one was being wishy-washy. Interesting.

When I think of what it means to be hip I focus on who defines that state of being. We don't generally ask octogenarians what's hip. Young people define what's hip. So when I think of hip, I think about what's appealing and magnetic from the point of view of young adults. Hipness at work, then, relates to our

---

1. Here's a link to that post about hipness on Management Craft: http://managementcraft
.typepad.com/management_craft/2007/03/do_you_need_to_.html.

FIGURE 2 **HIPNESS**

**HIPNESS
IN THE
WORKPLACE**

Communicate
•
Connect
•
Collaborate

**HIPNESS
IN THE
MARKETPLACE**

Enroll
•
Engage
•
Excite

abilities to be well regarded and sought out by young professionals. Here's my definition of hipness:

> **Hipness:** Our ability to communicate, connect, and collaborate with younger generations. In business, our hipness determines how effectively we work with, inspire, and influence younger workers. Hip entrepreneurs are able to enroll, engage, and excite younger customers and business partners.

As with the definition of sageness, I want to break down this definition because it contains several terms that deserve attention and clarification. Let's start with the terms used in the first sentence: *communicate, connect,* and *collaborate*—the three Cs of hipness in the workplace (see Figure 2).

THE THREE CS OF HIPNESS IN THE WORKPLACE

You are amazing and your sageness is valuable. Like buried treasure never found, it would be a shame if your knowledge and skills were not put to use helping the next generations grow and mature. Business acumen is a craft that is best learned through role modeling and mentoring relationships. The three Cs of hipness—*communicate, connect,* and *collaborate*—are all you need to ensure that your legacy can help others succeed.

COMMUNICATE

An overused term if there ever was one, the word *communicate* can mean many different things. At work, inadequate communication gets blamed for cultural ills and project failures. Managers attend $99 one-day training sessions touted as teaching communication skills. Communication is included on many performance evaluation forms, although the definition of what communication is varies on these forms and is often absent and left up to each manager and subordinate to figure out.

We could declare that communication is any message we impart—in any medium (face-to-face conversation, e-mail, signs, books, you name it). Using this definition, a leader who sends out lots of messages, talks a lot at meetings, and buys and hands out flavor-of-the-month management books like candy canes at Christmas would be considered a big communicator. And with this general definition, managers could call themselves hip if they sent lots of e-mails to younger workers. Don't scoff—this is a common strategy in organizations: Send more e-mail messages! Fill the in-boxes! I don't favor this definition of communication because it focuses solely on the act of sending information out and does not address how messages ought to be received. This is 50-yard-line communication, to use a football metaphor, because while you might have taken your message down your side of the field, you have not penetrated into the other person's territory and you are only halfway to your goal.

I hold communication to a higher standard and assert that it does not exist unless and until the message is received by the receiving party as it is intended by the sender. Using this definition, e-mail is communication only if the person reading it understands the information and interprets the tone and tenor as the author intended. If you send a vague message, it's not communication. If you send a message written in the wrong language for the receiver, it is not communication. If you write a ten-page report that no one reads or comprehends, you have not communicated. If you send an e-mail that ruffles a few feathers because the receiver thought you were angry when you were not, you have not communicated. Using this definition of communication, how many of the messages you send are received as communication?[2]

Compound this communication hurdle by adding a thirty-year difference in age between the sender and receiver, and communication becomes more challenging to accomplish because

---

2. As I was writing this book, I posted little bits and pieces on by blog, Management Craft, to get feedback and to see if the way in which I had written the piece resonated with people. This definition of communication is one such example. You can read the post and the comments here: http://managementcraft.typepad.com/management_craft/2008/03/communicate.html.

preferred methods and natural language patterns are likely dissimilar. As it relates to hipness, then, we communicate when messages are received by younger professionals in ways that they understand—when we come across as we intend to. This is an important distinction, and one that places the onus on us to find and use the best communication methods for our audience. Communication is the first of the three Cs of hipness and it is the bare minimum we should expect of ourselves in the workplace or in any professional setting.

CONNECT

When we connect with people, we relate based on common needs, goals, interests, or experiences. You and your best friends and family members will have many areas of connection, as would longtime coworkers. Two professionals from different functions, with different backgrounds, who are forty years apart in age, have fewer obvious connections. But just because the connections are not obvious, that does not mean they do not exist. On the contrary, it is easy to create a connection if you ask good questions and listen well. Hip and sage professionals actively seek conversations with younger professionals and quickly uncover common points of interest.

Like stitches bringing together two pieces of cloth, each connection strengthens the relationship.[3] It is our job to uncover and discover common interests, values, pet peeves, and

---

3. I am fascinated by the notion that there are no more than six degrees of separation between any two people. During his 1909 Nobel Peace Prize acceptance speech, Italian radio pioneer Guglielmo Marconi suggested that it would take only six relay stations to cover and connect the earth by radio. Marconi's work about our connectedness was the seed for the six-degrees-of-separation philosophy.

approaches to work. When we connect with colleagues our relationships improve in many ways:

- **Mutual respect.** Getting to know someone is an effective
  way to replace first impressions with accurate information.
  Until we connect, we base our judgments and opinions on
  observations and biases. After connecting with a younger
  colleague, we know more about the goals and interests we
  have in common.

- **Caring.** We care for people we know and who know us.
  Caring manifests in the workplace as consideration, coop-
  eration, attention, and assistance. A lack of caring manifests as apathy, avoidance, and combativeness.

- **Good judgment.** We make decisions every day. Our best
  decisions are well informed and considered. The more and
  better our relationships with younger professionals—who
  often have valuable perspectives different from our own—
  the better the decisions will be.

You do not need to become pals or golf partners to create a
connection. Professional connections are a basis of commonality
from which to appreciate diversity. Here are several easy techniques for improving connections with younger professionals:

- **Ask great questions.** Ask about projects. Ask for their
  opinions about vexing business problems. Ask them about
  their backgrounds. Ask them to explain new technologies
  you hear people talking about.

- **Eat in communal break rooms.** Do you eat your PB&J at
  your desk? Get out of your office and spend time where

people gather. Notice what people are talking about and get in on the conversation.

- **Don't be stingy with information about yourself.** We learn a lot about each other during small talk at the coffee machine. Develop your small talk skills and always greet people when you end up in the same spot—by the vending machines or copiers, at the reception desk, in the break room, or before or after meetings.

- **Show a genuine interest in others**. Ask follow-up questions to ensure you understand what the other person is saying.

- **Create a connection culture**. How numerous are the opportunities that employees have to network and share ideas? By scheduling informal conversation time and encouraging informal gatherings, you will create a culture that is more connecting. Be a participator at these gatherings. Ask a smart young professional to coffee once a month for an informal chat, and let your guest do most of the talking.

- **Volunteer to work on cross-functional projects.**

- **Seek alternative ideas and perspectives.** Don't be the older guy or older gal who is never receptive to new ideas.

Each of these techniques will help you get to know and care about your younger colleagues. Connections create an important context for both communication and collaboration. Communication is more likely to reach the receiver as intended when mutual respect and understanding exist between the sender and receiver. And it is easier and more enjoyable to collaborate with someone you know and trust.

COLLABORATE

Collaboration is the most difficult of the three Cs of hipness to practice. The first challenge, I think, is that many people don't know what good collaboration looks like, and they confuse collaboration with participation. I have known leaders who thought that allowing employees input constituted collaboration. Collaboration is not what happens when you ask for input and then use the input to make decisions. Collaboration is a creation by two or more individuals. When we collaborate, we work together to produce something—it is a joint activity. All collaborators own the outcome and all need to give up some control.

Many professionals say they want to increase collaboration, but few act consistent with this declaration. Our work habits, processes, and tools often do not reinforce or enable collaboration. We fill hour-long meeting agendas with a dozen topics, allotting only five minutes for each. We can't collaborate in five minutes. We ask training professionals to facilitate classes that cram three weeks' worth of learning into half-day or day-long sessions. We can't co-create a learning environment when topics are brushed over in forty-five-minute segments. We overbook our days with meetings and to-do list tasks. We can't create something together if we don't have the time to get together.

Think about the methods you use to manage and improve performance—do these methods facilitate collaboration? When we set goals, are they individual or team goals? When we fill out performance evaluations, do we emphasize team or individual performance? What criteria do we use for determining promotions, pay raises, and bonuses—individual or team accomplishments? I am not suggesting that reinforcing and acknowledging individual excellence is not a good thing—you should reinforce individual excellence. It is important, however, to notice the behaviors (competitive or collaborative) you are reinforcing.

People collaborate more when they are given the time, when it is easy to communicate with peers and team members, when they have had the opportunity to work with others, and when working together is a satisfying and fruitful experience. How many of these conditions exist in your work environment? As a hip and sage professional, you can help create the place for all these conditions.

Collaboration is as much a mind-set as it is a set of actions. When colleagues pool their ideas, thoughts, worries, and talents, they reinforce one another and help protect the team from setbacks. You want this natural process of synergy to flourish in your organization because it will serve you and your team well in times of struggle, pressure, or opportunity. Make sure your actions and words encourage effective collaboration with younger professionals. Here are questions you can use to kickstart situations that might be ripe for collaboration:

- Could you use some help on this project?

- Would you be willing to partner with me on this?

- If you were me, how would you approach this?

- What do you like about this idea (or opportunity, or project)?

- What ideas do you have?

- Who should be involved in this project, task, or initiative?

- What do I need to consider regarding technology?

- What do I need to consider regarding processes?

TABLE 1 **WAYS TO ENLIVEN HIP COLLABORATION**

CONTEXTUAL ELEMENT	FOR MORE HIP COLLABORATION
Physical location	**As an individual:** Be where the people you wish to collaborate with are. Locate yourself in the thick of things. Keep your office door open and be accessible. **As a team leader:** Seat teams together or in a way that encourages informal conversation. Make sure that you have informal meeting spaces available. If the team members are located in more than one place, make sure you get them together on a regular basis and they are encouraged to use technology to have informal as well as planned conversations. Make sure they have unrestricted access to phone, e-mail, Internet, teleconferencing services, and Web seminar software.
Communication processes	**As an individual:** Seek collaborators and give up control to allow co-ownership to flourish. **As a team leader:** Make it a habit to use a portion of your team meetings for collaboration. When people come to your office with questions or ideas, encourage them to gather together a few peers to talk it through—be a participant, not the boss.
Tasks and assignments	**As an individual:** Volunteer to work on group projects, especially those that will enable you to work with younger professionals. **As a team leader:** Assign projects and tasks to teams, subteams, and pairs of peers. Get your team members in the habit of working together.
Goals and measurements	**As an individual:** Negotiate goals that recognize collaboration. Develop your own definition of success that values collaborating with younger professionals. **As a team leader:** Make sure that at least half of your employees' goals are team, subteam, or pair goals. Use team measures along with individual measures for any evaluations, pay raise considerations, promotions, and bonuses.

TABLE 1 CONT'D

CONTEXTUAL ELEMENT	FOR MORE HIP COLLABORATION
Culture	**As an individual:** Be a model collaborator—open, engaged, flexible, and reliable. Thank people who collaborate with you.
	As a team leader: Reinforce and show appreciation for collaborative work. Model collaboration by asking team members and peers to work with you on your tasks and projects. Encourage diverse opinions and points of view. Show support when team members get together for informal conversations or meetings. Provide training and support. Talk about collaboration as a strategic strength.

- What do I need to consider regarding people?

- What do I need to consider regarding product?

- What should I do to ensure optimal benefit, value, and profitability?

- Should we be spending time on this?

No single question will lead to collaboration, but together they enliven business dialogue and create enrollment—a shared commitment to and interest in the project. Some work environments reinforce collaboration, but most do not. The workplace context is critical. Table 1 offers five methods you can use to improve workplace context and the odds for collaboration.

I like this suggestion for how to improve collaboration, from *Managing the Generation Mix* by Carolyn A. Martin and Bruce Tulgan:

If you really want to energize your team, throw away job descriptions and start from square one by dividing up tasks and responsibilities . . . ask them to divvy up assignments based on each one's talents and preferences. (2002, p. 109)

Assigning work based on strengths and interests is a winning strategy and I would fully support tearing up old job descriptions. Unnecessary and out-of-date job tasks suck up time and get in the way of collaboration.

Collaboration is not easy, but it is generally very rewarding. I have known several sage professionals who could not let go enough to allow another colleague into the project. Many of us are control freaks![4] We can get too comfortable with our job descriptions and functional silos—so comfortable that we have no room for collaboration. And often, our professional careers have been built on individual accomplishments and so this is what we know. Hip and sage professionals step out of the comfort zone and into the ambiguous and soupy world of collaboration.

First Impressions

First impressions are important and affect how well we will communicate, connect, and collaborate. Here's how two hip and sage professionals see it:

---

4. I know this because I am a recovering control freak. As a recovering control freak I have extrasensory perception and can spot a control freak from fifty feet away. Take it from me, while it is strange at first, it feels great to let go of the need to control. And besides, we are never really in control. Control is a sham that causes frustration and torment—for others and for us.

There has to be something about you that engages people to want to make eye contact with you, learn more about you, and exchange business cards with you. Consider the first impressions you are leaving— how you look then you open your mouth, how you speak, how you dress, and how you carry yourself. It doesn't make any difference if you're skinny or heavy, but if you don't present an honest picture of yourself or if you look old-fashioned you're not going to engage people. And so you need to be neat, clean, groomed, and have an up-to-date haircut.

Susan Ayers Walker

The twenty- and thirty-somethings have different val- ues and beliefs about work and life. The only way you're going to understand how to manage, how to connect with and be hip with them is to understand their perspectives, not to put them down. Why do they want to move so fast up the corporate ladder and what's occurring in the world that's affecting how younger workers act? Ask yourself: How do I feel about someone who has body piercings and tattoos? Am I putting up a wall or a bias because of a deeply held belief that I haven't been willing to let go of? I think we've got a responsibility; I think there are not enough folks connecting with this. Hipness and sage- ness is how do you draw people into life itself, into en- joying it, and how do you help them share learnings in a way that people embrace it, they value it, they love it, and they revel in it a bit.

Effenus Henderson

The three Cs of hipness are at the core of multigenerational success at work. If you want to improve your hipness so that

you can use your sageness, do whatever it takes—and that
might mean going beyond what's comfortable and familiar—to
reach out to, relate to, and work with the young professionals
within your organization.

> *If you want to relate to young people, you're not going
> to do it by saying, "When I was your age. . . ." Listen
> and ask questions about what's going on in their lives.*
> NANCY LEWIS

HIPNESS IN THE MARKETPLACE

Hip and sage entrepreneurs have an additional challenge: How
do I reach and work with younger customers and vendor partners? This is and will continue to be an important question. The
StartupNation blog offered this statistic:[5]

> *Since 2001, people ages 50–62 have been the fastest-growing
> group of new entrepreneurs in the U.S. In fact, according to
> the U.S. Small Business Administration, as of the end of
> 2006 53% of all American small businesses are run by an
> owner who is age 50 or over.* (Williams, 2007)

A 2006 article on Entrepreneur.com offered this compelling
tidbit regarding the businesses that Boomers are starting:[6] "And

---

5. You can find this post here: www.startupnation.com/blog/entry.asp?ENTRY_ID=619. The
StartupNation blog is a good resource for hip and sage entrepreneurs.

6. You can find the article here: www.entrepreneur.com/startingabusiness/article170206
.html.

just what kind of ventures are boomers starting? One very popular choice is online businesses" (Edelhauser, 2006). If you start an online business, you will definitely need to position yourself to market to and partner with younger professionals. So while you may be comfortable using the Internet to satisfy your needs, how comfortable are you that you know what you need to know to attract younger customers?

The final part of my definition of hipness addresses a fundamental need for hip and sage entrepreneurs—how do you enroll, engage, and excite younger customers and business partners?

ENROLL

Small businesses are finding and keeping customers using methods that center around relationships and stories. This is particularly true of online business practices. The price of entry for starting an online business is so low (relative to other start-ups) that millions and millions of people get on the Internet each year. This is why creating connections is so important. If we don't, we will not stand out—we'll be just a beige speck of sand on the world's largest beach.

Traditional marketing is out, and evocative and provocative storytelling is in. Spin is out, and transparency is in.[7] Static Web sites are out, and blogs are in. What do these pairings have in common? What's out involves being sold to, and what's in requires enrollment. What's the difference? When you sell people on an approach, they agree to do something in the manner you

---

7. *Transparency* refers to openness and candor. For example, if there were a blogger's code, one item would be that bloggers must reveal whether they are being paid to write about a particular topic. Sometimes bloggers are paid to write book or product reviews. Transparent bloggers always reveal any potential biases or conflicts of interest up front (not just in fine print, either). Transparent companies are upfront about product problems and how they will address them.

recommend—you have convinced them. That's great, and sometimes that would be your best possible outcome, but selling is not nearly as powerful as enrollment. When you enroll others, they take on the idea or approach as if it were their own. They become emotionally invested in the idea. They become evangelists for the program or project. Think **Apple.** Here are the activities you might do to sell or to enroll:

To sell:

- Offer information that supports your argument and recommendations—persuade with facts.

- Share your reasons—make your pitch.

- Detail features and benefits.

- Ask for agreement.

- Offer deals.

To enroll:

- Ask about and acknowledge needs, opportunities, current trends, and barriers. Create a common understanding for the current situation—warts and all.

- Offer information that goes beyond the brochure—share relevant information that enables others to see all sides of the issue and make their own conclusions. For example, it is no longer acceptable to have an impersonal "About Us" section on your Web site or blog. Your customers and partners want to know about you—the professional and the person.

- Invite customers into the product or service development process. Create collaborations with customers.

- Share your business goals and vision in a provocative and evocative way—tell your story with passion and commitment. If customers feel your passion, they will feel more connection to you and your company's products.

- Invite open and candid dialogue—have forums that enable customers to talk to you and other customers.

There is a big difference between these lists, isn't there? Enrollment requires connection and shared goals and values. As a business owner, you will need to open up and get real if you want to enroll customers and partners.

ENGAGE

Several of the techniques we use to enroll customers also serve to engage them. Even so, I think it is worthwhile to spend some paper and ink to address the power of engagement. To engage means to attract interest or attention so that people become involved. Traditional marketing techniques can be very effective at attracting interest and attention, but few cause customers to seek involvement in the company. When we engage our customers we connect with them to the point that they pull us into their lives. They become evangelists. Ideally, customers become co-creators, collaborators with us. Think of how different this is from the traditional customer–supplier model of doing business—the approaches are worlds apart.

Hip and sage entrepreneurs need to take time to learn and understand how the demand for transparency is changing how we do business. If you have or are going to start a business that needs a compelling online presence, spend time reading and learning about blogs and **wikis** and get to know the most popular **social networking** sites. Pay particular attention to Chapter 5, "New Technologies 101."

EXCITE

This element is easy to explain but hard to implement. Many great products fail to sell because they don't excite potential customers. If the problem is the product, it is time to rethink your business plan and value proposition. If the product is exciting but your approach to selling it is not compelling, that's an easier fix. The ultimate goal of **ProvoEvo** relationship marketing is for a product story to go **viral.** The post below describes what it means when something goes viral, but just know that it is something that is hard to manufacture. Viral marketing happens when customers and prospects get excited about your product. What excites people? Great stories. Fancy marketing copy and high-end stock photography cannot come close to the impact of a well-told (and retellable) story.

Going Viral

If you remember one particular shampoo commercial of the seventies, then you'll understand viral. In this commercial, the model "told someone, and then she told someone, and then she told someone . . . and so on and so on." The girl's face kept multiplying until the screen was filled. Viral marketing is nothing more than word-of-mouth marketing that is spread through the Internet. We've all gotten those chain e-mails from our well-meaning friends. "Forward this e-mail along to seven of your friends and something great will happen." If you have forwarded it, you've gone viral! You and your friends have generated buzz! We can't help ourselves. We want to share funny stories, provide advice, recommend good products, share the inside track, and come off as experts on almost everything. By tapping into the social networks, blogs, and video channels that your customers are visiting, you too can go viral.

Oprah Winfrey is a viral machine. Any product she mentions on her popular talk show becomes a best seller. The Internet enables this to happen on a grander scale because of immediacy. When Oprah mentions a book, millions of her fans go to Amazon.com and order it during the next commercial. The next day, people are buzzing about the show in the break room and then people go back to their work computers and order the book. If there were no Internet, lots of people would drive out to their local bookstore and buy the book, but not nearly as many. Here is just one example of Oprah's power to catalyze a viral movement, from the MSNBC Web site:[8]

> *More than one million copies of financial adviser Suze Orman's Women & Money have been downloaded since the announcement last week on Winfrey's television show that the e-book edition would be available for free on her Web site, for a period of thirty-three hours.* (Associated Press, 2008.)

But *how* do you get your message to excite and go viral? Here are some ways.

---

8. You can find this MSNBC.com article here: www.msnbc.msn.com/id/23208583/.

Be Read

Blog. Blogs are an excellent means of connecting in a very real way. The best blogs are honest, sometimes are humorous, and always reveal the true character of the person or brand. On Management Craft, my most popular posts are not necessarily the ones I think are most interesting or important—but they are almost always funny or sassy. Tame posts rarely go viral.

Be Heard

Podcast. If you have something interesting to say or if someone is saying something interesting about you, then consider podcasting. You can get your feed registered with all the major podcast search engines and uploaded to iTunes. My podcast series are by no means among the most popular, but I do get over 1,300 downloads a day, every day. I was sitting on a plane a couple of years ago and struck up a conversation with the person sitting next to me. Like me, he was a business consultant. He asked me my name and when I told him, he said he had one of my podcasts loaded in his iPod to listen to on this flight. Small world! Podcasts can be far-reaching.

Be Seen

Flickr site. Upload photos of yourself, or of your product being used in unusual ways. Anything that you can imagine can be found there. Among my favorites are the Jack in the Box "Jackball" photos that various members have uploaded.

YouTube. Upload videos that portray you or your product in an authentic way. If you don't believe me, consider the story of Tom Dickson, who started recording videos of the Blendtec blender chopping up the most outrageous items. The manufacturers claim that their sales have increased 500 percent since the start of these videos.

Be an Expert on a Social Network

Many social networking sites allow users to post questions and some allow users to rate the quality of the answers. If you are an expert on a particular subject, you can establish yourself as an authority by getting involved in topical user groups and sties. Some sites that offer this feature are **LinkedIn, Yahoo Groups,** and **AARP Groups.**

Be a Shameless Self-Promoter

Now, here's where the viral part comes in. After you've gotten your blog established or your Flickr account filled with photos, then get out there and share the news with all of your friends, family members, and even acquaintances. You'll tell them, then they'll tell someone, and so on and so on. Bloggers get e-mails every day from people they do not know asking to exchange a little link love. Don't do this unless you have something to say other than, *You have a business blog, I have a business blog, so let's exchange links with our readers.* We know you would not be making this request if you had readers, so why would an established blogger want to link to you? This approach is doomed to fail because it is not personal and interesting. If you want to get attention from other bloggers, write about their posts and link to them. Do it often and with sincerity. Write interesting posts that deserve attention. Link, write. Link, write. Repeat. This will earn you the coveted link love.

Tell a Story

I presented a **webinar** series for professional travel agents a few years ago. Provocative and evocative (ProvoEvo) online marketing was the topic of one sixty-minute webinar.[9] In particular, I talked with them about the power of enrolling, engaging, and exciting customers and prospects. A common pitfall is thinking that a great Web site is one with well-written content. Great Web sites have good content, but so do many mediocre Web sites. Good writing is easy to outsource. Great Web sites enroll, engage, and excite, and this is very different from what you find on a simply well-written site. To illustrate my point, I compared five Web sites from five tour companies that each sold biking trips through Tuscany. Looking at them individually, you would say that each site was well designed and attractive. The trips all sounded nice. And, most important, four of the five sounded exactly alike. Although they had different words, they all highlighted the rolling hills, fields of flowers, fine Tuscan wines, Pecorino dairy farms, walled cobblestone villages, and spirited locals. By the time you read about all four biking trips, you are confused and weary. Excellent writing is not enough! Everyone hires great writers.

The fifth Web site told a story that pulled you into the trip and introduced you to Luigi, a chef and fifth-generation farmer. Bikers who went on this trip would be meeting and dining with Luigi and his wife. This fifth company did not need to emphasize the rolling hills or the Pecorino cheese because customers

---

9. ProvoEvo: I think this is the secret formula for great storytelling. If you want to learn more about what it means to tell ProvoEvo stories, here is a link to a blog post I did about this in 2006: http://managementcraft.typepad.com/management_craft/2006/04/are_you _provoev.html.

who want to bike through Tuscany know they will experience these things. The moral of this story? It's about story! We should assume that our target customers will look up our Web site and the Web sites of other companies. If we have the same efficient writing as our competitors, we will not stand out.

PROVOEVO INSIDE OUTSIDE

Communication, connection, and collaboration. Enroll, engage, and excite. Both portions of my definition of hipness address a similar overriding theme, which is that if you want to build productive relationships with younger people, be prepared to open up and let go.

4

Tragically Hip

Sally was found in her fifth-floor condo, face down on her computer keyboard. An orange Goddard College hooded sweatshirt and blue Levis covered her body. A pair of $300 Bose headphones was stuck to her red, curly hair and ears. Her computer screen—still on—was filled with dozens of unanswered pop-up **IM** windows, and her **Skype** menu indicated that she had missed forty-seven calls. The last entry on her Twitter page read, "I'm out of Advil and my muscles ache something fierce. I need to order more from Amazon.com. Arrggh."

The coroner guessed that she had been dead for weeks. A few days prior, the police had received an anonymous phone call from someone who was worried that screen name BikerChic64 from Seattle might be in some kind of trouble. Detectives worked with computer technicians at the King County Crime Scene Unit to determine BikerChic64's real name and address.

The coroner ruled that Sally died from deep vein thrombosis. A clot from her leg moved into her lungs, killing her instantly. She had been sitting at her computer far too long.

Can we be tragically hip—hip to the point that it takes over our lives? Sadly, yes. Sally's story is extreme, but I have known many people who have gone off the deep end living in a virtual world. According to the American Association for Virtual Addictions (AAVA), the risks of developing a dependence on online communication tools are higher for older professionals because we can afford to buy more high-tech toys.[1] Don't let this happen to you. Here are a few symptoms that you might be headed toward technology dependence:

- To cut down on the wordiness of your PowerPoint slides, you have started using IM language at all your meetings. Your last presentation, titled ONRD404, was a hit with the new recruits.[2] Luckily, your boss did not pick up on what EMRTW meant.[3]

- You have an avatar named Wanda on **Second Life** who has taken over all your social responsibilities.[4]

- You have programmed your iPhone to wake you up in the middle of the night if you get pinged by one of your top five IM buddies.

- You ran into an old friend at Starbucks and shouted as you parted, "Let's hook up tonight—myspace or yours?"

---

1. The AAVA does not exist, although I would not be surprised if it popped up someday soon. Addiction to technology is a growing ailment, and with cool gadgets like the iPhone it will only get worse.

2. Our Numbers aRe Down and I don't know why.

3. Evil Monkeys Rule The World.

4. I know several professionals who have set up virtual meeting rooms in their virtual worlds. Their avatars meet to discuss real business problems and then tell their human equivalents what was decided. See it at http://secondlife.com.

- You maintain profiles at **Facebook, MySpace,** LinkedIn, **TeeBeeDee, 2People,** AARP, and **CycleSpace.**

- You spent $1,000 on **Woot** last month.

- You twitter every fifteen minutes and have five thousand contacts on your Twitter page.

- You write daily posts on your four blogs—one about chess, one about avatars, one about social networking sites, and one about virtual environmental projects.

- You have cashed out your SEP IRA to build a tech room.[5]

Lean back in your Herman Miller chair and pause. Is typing your only real activity at night? Do your online pals know you better than your spouse does? If so, you might need to go cold turkey for a few days to get the tech out of your bloodstream.

---

5. According to HGTV, tech rooms are very popular with Boomers. See "Boomer Trends: Flex Spaces and Tech Centers" at www.hgtvpro.com/hpro/di_design_trends/article/0,,HPRO_20174_4203348,00.html.

New Technologies 101

5

No book called *Hip & Sage* would be complete without a chapter about new technologies. The challenge is that technologies change faster than books flow through the publishing process. When planning this book, my editor and I talked about this chapter the most—how much to share, how much to emphasize, how to make sure it would be relevant on publication day.

And this is our challenge as hip and sage professionals, too, isn't it? Staying current requires constant attention and work. Just when we think we understand the latest technology, something new comes along. What's most important—for your professional success—is not that you understand X technology but that you are aware of technology and learn and use tech tools that will improve your ability to communicate, connect, collaborate, enroll, engage, and excite. My definition of hipness focuses on the relationships we build with young professionals because I know that if we build these relationships, our young colleagues will help us learn and use the technology tools that everyone is talking about.

I think this chapter is important for another reason, and that is to add to your technology vocabulary. I hated going to networking events or lunching in the break room and not knowing what people were talking about—I felt embarrassed. I opened this book with just such a story. So while some portion of the technologies mentioned in this section may be old news by the time you read it, my hope is that you will feel more comfortable talking about technology and—if you are new to this topic— you will not feel lost during lunchtime chats about the latest wiki Roger is showing off on his iPhone Web browser. For the up-to-date version of this chapter, see the "New Technologies 101" page at www.hipandsage.com.

I have selected nine technologies for this chapter—the ones that I think would be most helpful or interesting to hip and sage professionals. Between some of the technology reviews, I have sprinkled in advice and commentary from two very hip and sage professionals, Oliver Picher and Susan Ayers Walker.

> *I always keep a notebook with me so that if someone*
> *says something I know nothing about, I can write*
> *it down. When I get back home, I look up each of*
> *the topics on Google. It is a great way to learn.*
> SUSAN AYERS WALKER

BLOGS

Shorthand for the word *weblogs*, blogs are Web sites that employ specialized software to make adding and updating content quick and easy (many blogs are updated on a daily basis). They are often described as online journals featuring news articles and links to other blogs. The activity of writing and maintaining a blog is *blogging;* the author of a blog is called a *blogger,* and a blogger's articles are called **blog posts, posts,** or **entries.** Each entry is short—around two hundred words—and focuses on a single thought or topic (although post length varies from one line to thousands of words). Posts on a blog are almost always arranged in chronological order, with the most recent additions featured first. **Blogosphere** is a term describing the community of bloggers, their blogs, and how they are interconnected. The aggregators and the RSS feeds that notify readers when a blog has been updated are the things that make the whole system work and set a blog apart from a static Web site. In the following pages, you will learn more about RSS feeds and aggregators.

Best uses:

- Improving the flow of information among employees or customers. Many businesses are using internal blogs to share information and provide a forum for topic-focused discussion.

- Establishing yourself as a thought leader or expert. Since starting Management Craft, I have expanded my platform as a business consultant more than I could have done with my book and article writing.

- Marketing. Blogs provide another opportunity to communicate with your customers and illustrate the value your product or service offers.

- Staying current on a topic. My blog's readers keep me on my toes by challenging out-of-date perspectives and offering their thoughts and ideas to the conversation. As a blog reader myself, I read about what's happening right now. Most conferences, for example, have bloggers blogging about what's going on in each presentation as it is happening. Blogs often have details on breaking events before mainstream media outlets.

Why you should care/how to use:

- Blogs are a powerful tool to enliven and share your sageness. Most blogs are about a specific subject or topic and illustrate to readers that you have expertise in a particular area. What better way to share with your coworkers the knowledge you earned and the strengths you offer? Blogging is a great way to connect with others in the world who are looking for the information you are providing or who share a similar expertise.

- Blogs are a piece of cake to use—you do not need advanced computer skills to blog.

- Blogging improves the way you think and write. This has been the biggest benefit for me—my writing is much more engaging and personal than it was before I became a blogger (right?).

- As noted in "A Primer on the Generations," in the "Resources" section, blogs provide a valuable opportunity to connect with Millennials. Millennials seek a sense of community and they are eager to share their input and perspective on a solution. Blogs offer both of these aspects, not to mention being a great way to capture a lot of information and ideas in a short period of time.

Web sites where you can learn more:

- How to Blog: A Beginner's Blog Publishing Guide (www.masternewmedia.org/independent_publishing/ blogging-how-to-blog/guide-to-publishing-first-blog-20071104.htm.htm)

- Blog Search Engine (www.blogsearchengine.com)

- TypePad (www.typepad.com; this is a paid service, but it offers a thirty-day free trial)

There are lots of free blogging platforms, like blogger.com and Wordpress. I use and recommend TypePad because you can easily get up and running with a great-looking blog in minutes. I have had several blogs on TypePad and find it worth the cost.

One of the advantages of new media is that they allow you to test and see how different approaches might work. You could, for example, describe a product one way and see how your audience responds. Then you could describe the same product a different way, see how that works, compare the results, and then go back and use the description that worked better.

OLIVER PICHER

RSS FEEDS AND AGGREGATORS

Really Simple Syndication (RSS) is a format for notifying users when content has been updated on a subscribed list of Web sites, blogs, and podcasts. An *RSS feed* is how you receive an RSS document, which is called a *feed* or *channel* and contains either a summary of content from an associated Web site or the full text. An *RSS aggregator,* or *reader,* automatically checks your subscribed feeds regularly for content and downloads them to your computer or mobile device in a compact and useful manner. Producing an RSS feed is very simple, and millions of Web sites now provide this feature, including major news organizations like the *New York Times,* the BBC, and Reuters, as well most blogs.

Besides the many stand-alone aggregators, most Web browsers also have aggregators you can set up to collect and manage your RSS subscriptions. I use Net News Wire, which is a great product. If I were just starting out, however, I would probably use the aggregator that comes with Firefox, which is my favorite Web browser.

Best uses:

- RSS feeds brought together with an aggregator are a great way to get news and information. Your aggregator can select and sort stories from traditional outlets and blogs. It's like having a custom newspaper delivered every day that is being updated all day.

- I use RSS feed clusters for business training and development. Imagine if every employee had the ten best sites for their function on an aggregator that they reviewed each morning as they enjoy their first cup of coffee. All it would take is ten minutes a day to stay abreast of trends and developments in a particular field of work.

Why you should care/how to use:

- Anyone who uses the Internet as a main source of information should be aware of and use RSS feeds and aggregators.

- Here's an opportunity—ask younger colleagues which business sites they have in their aggregators. Not only will you establish a connection with each person, but you will find out what younger people are reading.

- Using RSS subscriptions and an aggregator, you can navigate through the online clutter and get to the information you need to achieve your professional goals.

- An aggregator saves you the time it would take to manually check each Web site to see if there is new content, and it allows you to have key information at your fingertips.

- As a business owner, publishing content by RSS feed allows you to stay in touch with customers.

Web sites where you can learn more:

- What Is RSS? RSS Explained (www.whatisrss.com)

- Bloglines, a Web-based aggregator (www.bloglines.com)

- Net News Wire (www.newsgator.com/Individuals/ NetNews Wire/Default.aspx)

> *Get on the computer and play games. If you find something that you want to do on the Web, something fun and interesting, you will also be learning to be more comfortable with the computer. You're learning how to manipulate and move between programs and*

the Internet. Each time you go back on the computer,
another learning lightbulb will go on and you'll have
acquired a little more skill. You'll feel more comfortable.
You won't feel like you're going to crash the thing.
SUSAN AYERS WALKER

INSTANT MESSAGING

Instant messaging, better known as IM or IMing in Internet slang, allows you to send real-time messages to individuals on your buddy or contact list. You type messages to each other into a small window that shows up on your screen and your buddy's screen. It is like a typed telephone call. Unlike with the telephone, you can have many IM conversations going on at once. This requires fast fingers and thinking, for sure, but don't be surprised if you see your granddaughter on her computer with five or six little dialogue windows open and going at once.

An IM buddy list allows you to track whether your buddies are online. Since instant messaging allows users to communicate in real time, users can respond quickly to questions or comments, making IM a faster and simpler way to communicate than e-mail. Much like texting, IMing has its own form of shorthand for quickly conveying a thought or emotion (for example, *btw* = by the way, *imho* = in my humble opinion, *lol* = laugh out loud).

Bear in mind that it is possible to pick up viruses, worms, and Trojan horses (these are all bad things) through IMing, so be cautious when you are accepting files. Also, don't type anything you don't want shared with others, since IMs can be captured and the text can be saved.

Best uses:

- Sending quick notes when a phone call is not practical or possible

- Communicating with virtual team members anywhere in the world

- Catching someone when you know they are available

- Practicing quick, abbreviated communication with younger workers

Why you should care/how to use:

- Imagine being on an important sales call and your customer asks a question that you don't know the answer to but Bob down the hall does. Instead of taking the steps to compose an e-mail (and he might not even be looking at his in-box), you can quickly type in the question as an IM, hit Send, and alert Bob to your question.

- IM will also allow your coworkers to tap into your knowledge quickly. Being available to Millennials and Gen Xers in a way in which they are accustomed to communicating can mean achieving better business results and connections.

- IM and text messages are a staple of communication for young professionals. The more you use IM, the better you will be able to use it at work. Ask your grandkids to get you set up for IM and text messages and to teach you how to use them—they will be thrilled to help!

Web sites where you can learn more:

- IM and text message dictionary of abbreviations (www.netlingo.com/emailsh.cfm)

- How Instant Messaging Works (http://communication
  .howstuffworks.com/instant-messaging.htm)

- Wikipedia, "Comparison of Instant Messaging Clients"
  (http://en.wikipedia.org/wiki/Comparison_of_instant_
  messaging_clients)

- Chat/SMS Text Messaging Shorthand, Acronyms & Emotions
  (www.shanemcdonald.com/laughs/l-SMS-Chat_Internet-
  Acronyms.html)

SOCIAL NETWORKING

Social networking allows individuals to connect with millions of individuals (online) rather than just the people they meet at school, in the workplace, or at a traditional networking event. Web 2.0 (the second generation of Web-based communities and hosted services) took social networking to a new level, with sites such as MySpace and Facebook opening up the possibilities for connecting with people who share similar interests or who may be good business contacts—or customers. Social networking Web sites also provide marketers with another opportunity to build relationships with customers and illustrate the value of a company's product or service.

Several social networking sites target older users. These sites connect mature adults and offer tailored content and networking opportunities. This might come as a surprise, but AARP.com, the Web site for the organization that used to call itself the American Association of Retired Persons, is pretty hip. Other social networking sites for sage people include TeeBeeDee, **Eons,** and **ThirdAge.**

You can find social networking sites for many interest groups—biker singles, chess aficionados, NASCAR fans. Harley-Davidson and many other companies have social networking on their Web sites to encourage customer connection, engagement, and loyalty.

Best uses:

- Recruiting employees. Business networking sites such as LinkedIn and Xing allow recruiters to find potential candidates and learn more about prospects before making contact.

- Customer service. The people who know your product best are the people who use it. That is the approach many companies are taking as they create social networking sites where customers can post answers to other customers' questions and, most important, provide you with invaluable feedback on your product or service.

- Improving the sales process. Companies are installing social network analysis software to reveal relationships among employees and with executives at other firms to help improve the sales process.

- Self-publishing and promotion. Social networking sites are a great way to share music, photos, and videos—and when it comes to promoting or marketing yourself, they can be a powerful tool for potential job and sales opportunities.

Why you should care/how to use:

- It's important to be where your customers are, so if your clients (or your coworkers) are using social networking, it's time to start building your own online network.

- If you are looking for a new job opportunity, you will want to create a profile that outlines your experience and expertise. This is a great way to ensure recruiters will find you rather than waiting for them to go through the stack of résumés on their desk or in their e-mail inbox.

- Social networking is the perfect tool for testing out the six-degrees-of-separation theory. Once you have established a profile on a couple of sites and have built your network, you will find that you are just a few connections away from many of the people you might want to contact.

- Facebook and MySpace are very popular with young people, so you need to understand what these sites look like and how they connect people.

Web sites where you can learn more:

- AARP (www.aarp.org/onlinecommunity)

- TeeBeeDee (www.tbd.com)

- ThirdAge (www.thirdage.com)

- Eons (www.eons.com)

- LinkedIn (www.linkedin.com)

- Facebook (www.facebook.com)

- MySpace (www.myspace.com)

- Social Networking Technology Boosts Job Recruiting (www.npr.org/templates/story/story.php?storyId=6522523)

- Why You Shouldn't Ignore Social Networks (www.socialcustomer.com/2007/01/why_you_shouldn.html)

- Should Your Organization Use Social Networking Sites? (www.techsoup.org/learningcenter/internet/page7935.cfm)

Plunge in and start experimenting with new media rather than getting too intellectual about it. Go in and start up a personal Facebook or a MySpace page or start your own blog. Experience these communication methods and see how comfortable you are with how they work. If you don't feel like starting a blog yourself, start reading blogs. Get to know the bloggers and the people who are commenting and make comments yourself until you are comfortable with the ebb and flow of conversations that are happening online.

OLIVER PICHER

WIKIS

Ward Cunningham, designer of the first wiki, called it "the simplest online database that could possibly work." A wiki is an open, collaborative Web site where users and contributors can add, remove, and edit content using a Web browser. Wikis' open editing feature allows you to collect valuable information from anyone willing to share knowledge with you. It's especially helpful when you want to exchange information between and within teams. Wikis are easy to use and maintain—they don't require administrative effort, and content can be updated quickly; users and contributors can simply visit and update the Web site at any time.

The most famous wiki is **Wikipedia**—the online encyclopedia. It is important to note, however, that because a wiki can be changed and updated by anyone, the validity of the content is not guaranteed. In chapter 4 I wrote about the importance of letting go of control when working with talented younger people. A wiki is a great business tool for hip and sage professionals, but be prepared to give up control.

Best uses:

- Personal note taking, organization of information

- Collaborating with coworkers online or managing a group project

- Creating an internal knowledge base

- Assembling an online community

- Managing a traditional Web site

Why you should care/how to use:

- As with a blog, you don't need to be technically savvy to create a wiki.

- Wikis allow you to solicit feedback and expertise from coworkers and find it all in one location. What better way to hear from employees than in their own words?

- Wikis can help you manage projects.

- Because wikis are open-source code, they are free to companies who opt for an open-source distribution, or relatively cheap for companies willing to pay for their implementation and support.

- Wikis can centralize information in many formats, such as spreadsheets, Word documents, PowerPoint slides, PDFs— anything that can be displayed in a browser.

Web sites where you can learn more:

- Wikipedia (www.wikipedia.org)

- **Wikispaces** (www.wikispaces.com)

- **Wet Paint** (www.wetpaint.com)

- What Is a Wiki (www.oreillynet.com/pub/a/network/2006/ 07/07/what-is-a-wiki.html)

- Google Sites (www.google.com/sites/#utm_campaign = en&utm_source=en-ha-na-us-google&utm_medium = ha&utm_term=wiki%20projects)

> *Like it or not, as we get older we become slightly disabled in many areas. We lose dexterity in our hands because of arthritis. After about the age of forty-five we lose our hearing because we had our nine-transistor radios when we were young, and our Sony Walkmans. I'm sixty and I wear trifocals, for God's sake. My flexibility, my response time, is not as sharp as it used to be—and I feel it especially when I'm playing games and get outfoxed by the younger set. But I still play.*
> SUSAN AYERS WALKER

VOIP

VoIP, or voice-over-Internet protocol, is changing the way we place and receive phone calls by turning analog audio signals into digital data that can be transmitted over the Internet. VoIP software allows you to turn a standard Internet connection into a way to make calls, essentially bypassing the phone company and its charges. This technology also benefits corporations because VoIP allows them to maintain one network instead of two, one for phone and one for data.

Skype is one of the most popular VoIP providers as it lets you make free calls over the Internet to anyone else who also has the service. It's free and easy to download and use, and it works with most computers. I love Skype and use it to chat with people all over the world for free. I have one client who uses Skype for business communication between offices.

It used to be that VoIP phone service was available only from computer to computer. But now, VoIP phones are available, allowing you to use VoIP technology on a handheld phone that's not connected directly to a computer.

Best uses:

- Making free or inexpensive phone calls to anywhere in the world (except for the price you pay for your Internet service)

- Reducing complexity for IT departments, which need to maintain only one network instead of separate networks for voice and data

- Easy conference calling, recording, and sharing of files during the conversation

Why you should care/how to use:

- If your clients or coworkers are using VoIP, it's important to understand and use this technology to communicate and connect with them.

- Using VoIP can save you money and improve your company's bottom line.

- If you come in on Monday morning and tell your younger colleagues that you spent the weekend Skyping with pals from around the world, you will firmly establish yourself as hip and sage.

Web sites where you can learn more:

- Skype (http://skype.com)

- How VoIP Works (http://communication.howstuffworks .com/ip-telephony. htm)

PODCASTING

Podcasts are audio segments delivered via RSS feed to iPods and other portable media players. Many people think that a podcast is any audio recording accessible on the Internet, but technically a recording is not a podcast unless it is available by RSS feed. Podcasts are easy to share and distribute.

I have a series of business conversations that I distribute by RSS feed.[1] You can find my podcast on iTunes, various other podcast sites, and my blog and Web site. It took some work to set up the RSS feed and to make it available on iTunes and other podcast sites, but once this was set up, I did not need to worry about distribution again.[2] Podcasts can be displayed on Web

---

1. My podcast series is called "Fireside Chats About Management and Leadership." You can find my complete library of podcasts on iTunes or on my Web site: www.lisahaneberg.com/ podcasts-and-webcasts.

2. I hired someone to get the RSS feed for my podcasts listed on all the big sites. If you are giving podcasting a try for the first time, you might want to hire a contractor to help you get things set up and teach you the basics.

sites with clickable links to audio files, typically in MP3 format.

To get set up to podcast you need a way to record the podcast (I use **Audacity** software and a **Dynametric** device that connects my phone to my computer). You also need a place to upload, store, and publish podcast episodes (I use a site called **Hipcast**).

Best uses:

- Training—instructional informational materials

- PR—promoting your services

- Knowledge sharing—providing valuable resources and information to associates and clients

- Self-guided walking tours—informational content

- Music—band promotional clips and interviews

- Talk show formats—industry or organizational news, investor news, sportscasts, news coverage and commentaries

Why you should care/how to use:

- Podcasts allow you to choose your own programming and listen to it whenever and wherever is most convenient for you.

- Creating a podcast that informs associates and customers about what's going on with your business can be a great and easy way to promote your business, your interests, and your areas of expertise.

- Listening to podcasts can expand your knowledge—even when you're at the gym.

Web sites where you can learn more:

- Audacity (http://audacity.sourceforge.net)

- Dynametric (www.dynametric.com)

- Hipcast (www.hipcast.com)

- **Podcast Alley** (www.podcastalley.com)

- **PodcastBunker** (www.podcastbunker.com)

- **Podcasting Tools** (www.podcasting-tools.com)

- Why Podcast? (www.podtopia.net/articles/whypodcast .shtml)

WEBINARS

Webinars—slang for *Web conferences* or *Web meetings*—allow you to conduct live sales meetings, presentations, seminars, and ad hoc meetings over the Internet. Webinar participants join the meeting from their computer anywhere in the world through the Internet. Webinar presenters can solicit as little or as much audience interaction as desired. Participants see and hear the presentation. Participants can also share and view any files on their computers, making this an ideal technology for project update meetings and virtual collaboration.

Because the presentation is not in person, webinars should be short or participants will get bored and start handling e-mail and other tasks instead of paying attention (this is a risk regardless of the length).

Best uses:

- Communication and connection for dispersed teams

- Building better relationships with customers while lowering travel costs

- Reaching a larger audience during product launches and press conferences

- Working with a team or multigroup project

- Providing short, cost-effective training

Why you should care:

- Workplace boundaries have expanded, meaning workers no longer work in the same office building, city, or even country. Web conferences provide a great way to connect with individuals—all participants are able to share and view documents and displays in real time.

- Whether you are working with a potential client or a team, Web conferencing gives you another tool to help close the deal or move forward on an important project.

- Webinars provide an effective method for training people and making sales presentations. Sharing PowerPoint presentations, documents, and even applications is easy, as are multiparty videos and virtual whiteboards.

Web sites where you can learn more:

- **Go To Meeting** (https://www1.gotomeeting.com)

- **WebEx** (www.webex.com)

- **Live Meeting** (http://office.microsoft.com/en-us/livemeeting/ FX101729061033.aspx)

- **Great Web Meetings** (www.greatwebmeetings.com)

- **Acrobat Connect Professional/Personal Web Conferencing** (www.adobe.com/products/acrobatconnect/)

In marketing, when people ask me whether understanding technology is important, I always turn the question around and ask them about their buyers—where are their customers and where would their customers expect to find them? You need to communicate with your buyers the way they prefer, not the way you prefer. If you want to reach people who use new media to communicate, then you need to be there— and you need to be using viral marketing to reach them.

OLIVER PICHER

IPODS AND MP3 PLAYERS

MP3s, which are compressed audio files, changed how we listen and share music and created a market for MP3 players such as Microsoft's **Zune** and the popular iPod. With an MP3 player, you can create personalized music lists and carry thousands of songs wherever you go.

The iPod is a small handheld media center with a digital audio player, video player, photo viewer, and portable hard drive. Now in its sixth generation, the iPod classic allows you to play songs, movies, games, and photo slideshows as well as store up to 160GB. Sure, there are other MP3 players, but the iPod is king. And since I have made no claim of objectivity, I will admit to being an iPod junkie—I have three!

iTunes is the integrated jukebox and media player software that comes with an iPod. It lives on your computer, and you use it for organizing, playing, converting, and downloading files from an external source to your computer and from there to your player.

Best uses:

- Corporate training! Yes, I think training departments ought to hand out iPods like they do laminated IDs. iPods are a wonderful delivery system for training podcasts and video-casts.

- Listening to music, audiobooks, and podcasts

- Watching archived TV shows

- Organizing and condensing your entire music collection

Why you should care:

- An iPod reduces clutter—you can download all those CDs lying around to your iTunes library, one central location where you manage your music.

- You can buy single songs rather than having to buy the en-tire CD.

- It comes in handy on a short bus ride or long plane ride as you can listen to audiobooks, get caught up on podcasts and your favorite TV shows, and listen to music.

- Nearly everyone under the age of eighty has at least one iPod, so you should have one, too.

Web sites where you can learn more:

- Apple (www.apple.com)

- Zune (www.zune.net/en-US)

- **Fifty fun things to do with your iPod**
  (www.kottke.org/plus/50-ways-ipod)

NEWER, BETTER, COOLER

Technologies change in two ways—with brand-new inventions and with iterations of the old. Most of the time, the latest thing is a new, better, and cooler version of something that came before it. I hope you found that this chapter helped increase your awareness of the types of technologies that are popular and useful in a business setting.

Hip

&

Sage

Charlie Rose on Your iPod

Some people find the term *juxtaposition* (placing two things or ideas next to each other) pretentious, but I think it's delicious. Hip and sage professionals juxtapose regularly and vigorously. Imagine two worlds being ripped apart and smooshed back together again. Like shifting continental plates, juxtaposed topics and conversations create new vistas. The concept of hip and sage is an example of juxtaposition—and you can get better at being both hip and sage by putting more juxtaposition in your life. Here are four varieties of hip and sage juxtaposition and several suggestions for how to use these methods.

A SCREW CAP ON WHAT???

The $135 bottle of wine with a screw cap asks us to revisit other previously pooh-poohed methods. In the past, screw caps have been synonymous with cheap wine. Unfortunately, the more accepted high-end bottle closure—the corks—has high spoilage rates. Corks go bad, they crumble, and many do not fit the bottle properly and allow air to get in. Approximately 15 percent of wines in corked bottles eventually spoil due to bad corks. In 1997, Plumpjack Winery began bottling half of its $135/bottle Reserve Cabernet Sauvignon with screw caps (the other half had the traditional corks). Many in the wine community found this an outrage, but some thought it a wonderful revolution whose time was inevitable. This intense and rich wine, with notes of plum and cedar and nutmeg, has consistently received excellent ratings from *Wine Spectator* magazine—in both cork and screw cap. Now screw caps are gaining broader acceptance as a good alternative to cork.

So, in the screw-cap approach, methods you tried and rejected ten years ago might be worth trying again in the current context. The people are different, the circumstances are different, the tools are different—the results will be different, also. Why not take the initiative to talk about the methods you have considered over the years? You are the keeper of history and in the best position to ensure that your current team members don't reinvent previously explored opportunities. One caveat about using the $135-bottle-of-wine-with-a screw-cap method: share the ideas without judgment. Never say, "We tried that and it didn't work"; say, rather, that these are methods that you tried and that might be worthy of reconsideration. If a winery can put a screw cap on an expensive and delicate Cabernet Sauvignon, anything is possible. Fresh circumstances can make dusty ideas shine again.

YOU GOT THAT WHERE???

The drive-through caviar stand also is a very useful image for hip and sage professionals. Many of us have developed a sixth sense about the finer aspects of work. We have business acumen for quality and decision making, and we are good judges of talent. These days, however, talent might be wrapped up in an electric blue–haired, lip-pierced, and forearm-tattooed package. When we use the drive-through-caviar-stand method, we expect quality while embracing contemporary methods of delivery.[1] Hire the brilliant candidate with a spiky Mohawk hairdo who spent his summers as a roadie for the hard rock band Korn instead of interning with one of the Big 5 accounting firms.[2] Relax a bit on how things are done, not on whether they are done well. Be flexible with how meetings are conducted, not with the quality of the conversation. Let people create a workplace they find comfortable and pleasing, but ensure that the culture reinforces excellence. Be forceful and emphatic when you talk about your intent and less so when weighing alternatives that support goals.

CHARLIE ROSE HOW???

This next method of juxtaposition helps us become and stay hip in the workplace. Do you like classical music? Is Hemingway

---

1. While I was not able to find an actual caviar drive-through stand, readers who find they need to quickly satisfy their love of caviar can try www.911caviar.com, where sixteen ounces of Russian Imperial will set you back only $1,840. All orders over $500 include free shipping.

2. Although the Mohawk hairstyle is named after the Mahican and Mohawk Native American tribes, some believe that the hairstyle was actually worn by the Wyandot tribe, who

your favorite author? Do you favor fountain pens over purple gel stick pens? Is Charlie Rose your favorite interviewer? Our level of interest in our favorites is always high, so why not use this energy to learn about new technologies? Would you like to learn about blogs, podcasts, e-books, and wikis? No problem! Combine it all together using the Charlie-Rose-on-your-iPod method of juxtaposition. Fill your screaming-hot red 160GB video iPod with Beethoven and podcasts of the *Charlie Rose* program.[3] Find blogs about Hemingway and fountain pens. Experiment with a wiki to catalog your classical favorites. Download Hemingway, Steinbeck, and Louis L'Amour onto your Kindle e-book reader.[4] Find Billy Joel's MySpace page. Set up a Google group for your bridge club. You don't need to change your tastes to learn about new media. Ask a younger colleague to sit with you for thirty minutes and show you how to find your favorites using new media. You can also use the Charlie-Rose-on-your-iPod method to communicate, connect, and collaborate with younger workers. Be like Charlie Rose and podcast or videocast your business updates. Take a page from the Billy Joel playbook and set up an internal social network on your company's intranet. Create a blog for your department that enhances information sharing, informal conversations about top-of-mind topics, and quick dissemination of training and reference materials.

---

were misidentified by French explorers. The oldest known Mohawk hairdo belonged to the 2,300-year-old Clonycavan Man—a male bog body found near Dublin, Ireland.

3. If you go to www.charlierose.com you can subscribe to the RSS feed for the *Charlie Rose* program and have your favorite interviewer show up automatically each time you plug your iPod into your computer and fire up iTunes. You can fit up to two hundred hours of Charlie Rose video on your 160GB iPod.

4. Yes, I am biased. Sony has an e-book reader too (and maybe more by the time you read this), but it does not hold a candle to the Kindle e-book reader, in my humble opinion. The Kindle allows you to buy and instantly download books from Amazon.com anywhere in the United States, without a WiFi signal. Even Hemingway, Steinbeck, and Louis L'Amour!

WHO'S ON MTV???

The Tony-Bennett-plays-MTV method is perhaps the most help-ful and easily implemented method of professional juxtaposi-tion.[5] Tony Bennett is a legend.[6] We are legends, too. If, in an effort to be hip, Tony Bennett sang Britney Spears songs, it would be a tragedy for all involved. Sixty-somethings who act like twenty-somethings look ridiculous. So should we resign ourselves to playing bridge on Wednesday afternoons with the semiretired folks down the street? No! We can behave consis-tently with our age and be totally hip. When Tony Bennett sang on *MTV Unplugged* in 1994, he crooned his way into the young audience's heart. He did not change who he was or act unchar-acteristically; he just went where the young people were and did his thing—and he was amazing! The Tony-Bennett-plays-MTV method is all about context.

Is your environment provocative and evocative? In the In-troduction, I shared a story about how I had an epiphany about blogging at a *Fast Company* readers network gathering. Had I stayed at home that night, I might never have learned about blogging. If you want to communicate, connect, and collaborate with younger workers, be where they are. Croon if you are a crooner, but do so at Starbucks while sipping a soy vanilla latte. The Tony-Bennett-plays-MTV method also relates to how and

---

5. Tony Bennett played on *MTV Unplugged* on April 15, 1994. Contemporary (at the time; now they too might be considered hip and sage) stars Elvis Costello and k.d. lang sang duets on the show.

6. Tony Bennett has a MySpace page at www.myspace.com/tonybennettmusic. If you look on his friends list, you will find hip young folks like Diana Krall, but you will also find folks like Andy Williams. Yep, Andy Williams has a MySpace page, too. Find it at www.myspace .com/andywilliamsmusic and learn more about MySpace while listening to *Moon River.*

where we get information. It's OK if you love reading *Forbes*, the *Wall Street Journal*, and *Harvard Business Review*—these are fine publications all. You can improve your hipness, however, by also reading *Fast Company*, *Wired*, *Ode*, *Slate*, and the *Onion*. Here's how hip and sage professional Nancy Lewis keeps current:

> *I have two daughters in their twenties and they keep me up-to-date on music and movies and things like that. I read a lot, I watch a lot of—I was gonna say news—Jon Stewart.[7] I visit a lot with young people at church and I'm a Leadership Austin alumna, where I'm one of the many seniors in that group, but it's great to mingle with different age groups. I am the senior listening to them and talking to them, learning from them. Lifelong learning is critical to staying hip.*

What would be the equivalent of *MTV Unplugged* in your workplace? Be there. Hip and sage juxtaposition offers us new ways to mix up, spice up, and splice up our work. Life is full of fragments that come together—sometimes in strange and magical ways—to define our experiences and fuel our curiosities. As you read chapter 5, keep these methods of juxtaposition in mind; they might give you new ideas for ways to enliven your hipness.

---

7. *The Daily Show* with Jon Stewart. Find it here: www.thedailyshow.com. You can buy *Daily Show* episodes and have them delivered by RSS feed to your iPod through iTunes (if you have not already filled it with *Charlie Rose* episodes).

7

Your Definition of Success

Recognizing what it means to be sage and to get hip is not enough; you still need to bring these two diverse worlds together. If you endeavor to be and remain hip and sage, you will want to align how you define success to support your goals.

Do you remember how you defined success when you were twenty-five years old? Depending on your circumstances at that time, you probably defined job success in terms of promotions, money, stability, fancy job titles, assigned parking spaces, and company cars. Most of us were driven by a need to look good and be recognized for our individual accomplishments at age twenty-five. And while recognition and ego may still be important drivers decades later, other needs and interests have changed how we define success. Hip and sage professional Nancy Lewis had this to say about how her definition of success has changed over the years:

> *Twenty or thirty years ago, I dwelled on and defined the*
> *success of my work based on how hard I could work, how*
> *much I could complain about how hard I was working, how*

much I could complain about how stupid people were and how things would be better if they only did it my way. I am so grateful I lived through and outgrew those stages! Today, I define success as those moments where people enjoy things I've written or where I enjoy what I've written, produced, or am adding to the corporate dialogue. I get great kicks out of that and I realize that the most important accomplishment is the one I can accept and experience— I do not need somebody else to notice it.

As Nancy's comment highlights, one of the other dimensions of our definition of success that changes is how we assign meaning to events and actions. It is common for young professionals to overassign meaning to small incidents. The first time someone was criticized by their boss in a meeting was probably a devastating experience—it can seem like the end of a career! Add thirty years of experience and this same situation feels like a normal part of spirited work dialogue. Shifts in how we define success as we age are normal and helpful. For hip and sage professionals, understanding how definitions of success develop and change can heighten both sageness and hipness.

BELIEFS, ACTIONS, RESULTS, AND SUCCESS

Your definition of success is the collection of beliefs you hold that influence your goals and priorities, and that determine your actions and results. These beliefs affect the decisions you make, the activities you favor, and those you avoid.

FIGURE 3 **THE BELIEFS–ACTIONS–RESULTS CYCLE**

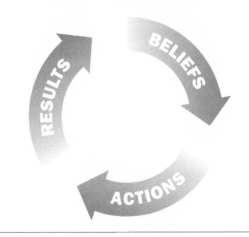

There is a direct relationship between beliefs and actions. Actions come from beliefs, and actions and results reinforce beliefs (see Figure 3, the Beliefs–Actions–Results Cycle). This cycle can work either for or against your success. By adopting beliefs that serve our goals and priorities, we will enjoy life more fully and succeed more.[1] Table 2 illustrates the connection between beliefs and behaviors.

Your definition of success is made up of many beliefs:

- Beliefs about how success is achieved

- Beliefs about what success looks like

- Beliefs about what is expected of you

---

1. You can use the Beliefs–Actions–Results Cycle in reverse to diagnose reasons why results are lacking: What were the results? What actions did I take that led to these results? What beliefs or assumptions led to my choosing these actions? You can also use it to look forward and evaluate alternative approaches to a new project and to determine if you should shift your beliefs to achieve your goals: What are my fundamental beliefs about this project? Given these beliefs, what actions am I likely to take? Will these actions produce the results I seek?

TABLE 2 **BELIEFS THAT CAN LEAD TO BEHAVIORS**

BEHAVIOR	WHAT BELIEFS MAY HAVE LED TO THIS BEHAVIOR?
Always comes to meetings on time	• Professionals show up to meetings on time. • It is important to respect the time of others. • I am expected to be on time. • If I am late, I will miss something.
Is always late to meetings	• Everyone is always late. • It is not important to be on time. • My timetable is more important. • I will not miss anything; this is not worthwhile. • Nobody cares if I am late. • I am too busy to be on time.
Is defensive when being given feedback	• I need to prove that I am right. • People who are weak need input and help. • I look bad when others challenge my ideas. • I need to win to feel good. • I do not value the other person's input. • I am embarrassed when challenged in public.
Micromanages	• I am expected to stay on top of the details. • If I do not check up on them, they will not complete the work to my satisfaction. • My employees cannot be trusted. • My employees constantly need my help. • This is what good management looks like. • I would rather work with my employees doing these tasks than spend time doing other tasks.

TABLE 2 CONT'D

BEHAVIOR	WHAT BELIEFS MAY HAVE LED TO THIS BEHAVIOR?
Does not share input in meetings when the agenda is known ahead of time	• I prefer to think things through before commenting. • If he wants my opinion, he will ask me. • I do not want to stick my neck out by sharing my ideas. • This is not my meeting; I am not the leader. • I am not expected to contribute in this meeting.
Regularly discusses ideas and issues with manager	• I am expected to form and share ideas and issues. • My manager wants to hear from me. • I need to make sure my manager knows about the key issues within my area. • Employees should toot their own horn to get noticed.
Communicates with manager only when asked and only on topics asked about	• When it comes to my manager, no news is good news. • Managing on my own is a sign of strength; asking my manager to review what's going on shows that I am weak and need help. • My manager is too busy to talk to me; I am not a priority.
Avoids coaching others	• If I talk to these people, it will make things worse between us. • The discomfort of the conversation will outweigh any benefits. • They will come around on their own. • I have too many tasks to do that are more important. • I don't want to do this. • Young people don't listen.

TABLE 2 CONT'D

BEHAVIOR	WHAT BELIEFS MAY HAVE LED TO THIS BEHAVIOR?
Resists changes suggested by younger professionals	• Young people have not yet learned enough to have good ideas. • I am afraid of their newfangled ideas. • It will change back to the old way; it always does. • There is nothing wrong with the way things are.

- Beliefs that have been reinforced by past successes and failures

- Comparative assumptions about the actions and circumstances that have led to other people's success

- Beliefs, whether positive or negative, handed down by your role models

As a hip and sage professional, you will find it helpful to regularly evaluate and realign the beliefs that lead to your definition of success, which you'll have the opportunity to do later in this chapter. And although how you define success will change as a normal part of the saging-up process, you can accelerate this process to serve your goals and priorities more effectively.

The process of aligning your definition of success can be tricky because it's common not to know or recognize some beliefs that are key drivers of behavior. People often verbally define success as one thing and then behave in a contrary way. For example, a leader might say that success means achieving results for the benefit of the company and its employees while behaving in ways indicating that success really means being right and in control.

To develop the capacity to recognize the beliefs that make up your definition of success, complete Worksheet 1. Write down five recent actions and ask yourself, What beliefs led to these actions? Be wary of your natural inclination to define logical reasoning as the belief that led to your actions. Any action has many potential beliefs behind it, so it is best to identify the possibilities and then select the correct motive. Table 2 offers several examples for you to use as a starting point.

I find it fascinating to think about how beliefs fuel behaviors and how we change. Change occurs after we adjust our beliefs. Are you habitually late to meetings? You might figure you are late because you are busy and not think much more about it than this. But there is more to it. Other people are busy, too, and many of them manage to make it to meetings on time. What do on-time people say to themselves that is different from what late people say to themselves? Do you like the attention you get

WORKSHEET 1 **BELIEFS LEADING TO BEHAVIORS**

BEHAVIOR	WHAT BELIEFS MAY HAVE LED TO THIS BEHAVIOR?

from being late? Do you believe that meetings are a waste of your time? Do you think that your time is more valuable than other people's time? What would happen if you took on the belief that it is rude and irresponsible to habitually be late and that lateness reflects poorly on your ability to manage your time and work?[2]

Here's another example. Whether and how we approach and partner with younger professionals is affected by our beliefs about them. Do you admire the skills of young people? Do you feel threatened by younger employees? Do you believe that young people don't have a good work ethic? Do you believe that everyone should pay their dues, work their way up the corporate ladder, and wait their turn to take key leadership roles? Your answers to these and many other questions will affect how you interact with younger employees and the strength of your relationships with them.

Does your current definition of success enhance your sageness and hipness? I have talked to and worked with many hip and sage professionals and find they share many beliefs. These, along with their other beliefs about goals and priorities, come together to shape their definitions of success.

HIP AND SAGE BELIEFS

I first started formulating this list of hip and sage beliefs a few years ago. The beliefs that made the list are ones I heard again

---

2. If you struggle to be on time at work, you might enjoy a post on the *Fast Company* blog from September 2004. Here is the link: http://blog.fastcompany.com/archives/2004/09/08/late_to_work.html.

and again. In addition, I received nearly complete agreement on two topics—relevancy and learning. I have asked hundreds of mature professionals if they had ever felt irrelevant. I expected almost everyone to say that they had, but the hip and sage professionals responded that they had never felt irrelevant. The professionals that were not yet sage almost always had experienced times at which they felt irrelevant. I was blown away by this clear difference and pondered the classic chicken-and-egg conundrum—which came first, hipness or the feeling of relevancy? Here is how hip and sage professional Robert Levit answered my question of whether he had ever felt irrelevant:

Gee, I hate to admit this, but I really haven't felt irrelevant. I plainly perceive—in my classes, my interactions with businesspeople and community leaders, and from diverse groups of people—that what I have to offer is relevant. But I think the obligation to communicate that within the current social context is mine. It is my job as an educator to communicate universal principles, best practices, and my personal experiences in ways that contemporary people can use. I feel more relevant now than ever. I have from time to time questioned my own abilities to communicate within a contemporary context— but that's a matter of practice, not a function of relevance.

Relevancy is an important DNA-like marker of hipness because when we feel we can make a contribution, we seek ways in which to do so successfully. Something is relevant when it is appropriate to the matter at hand. Professionals are relevant when the work they do fits the needs of—is appropriate to— their current organization. I think that when we believe that the work we do is relevant, we are more likely to actively seek ways to communicate, connect, and collaborate with other professionals.

A passion for and acceptance of lifelong learning is another key DNA marker for hip and sage professionals.[3] Hip and sage professionals accept the fact that lifelong learning is a must—it's part of the price of entry into a vital and vigorous life. Interestingly, this matter-of-fact acceptance is almost always coupled with a deep passion for learning. Hip and sage professionals take classes, ask younger workers for coaching, attend conferences, and read voraciously. I have met fifty-year-olds who have not yet learned how to use e-mail and eighty-year-olds who download

Beliefs That Enhance Sageness

- Lifelong learning is fun and important.

- I have learned a lot but have just as much to learn.

- My skills and experiences are relevant and valuable, and I can make a contribution.

- It is OK to downsize and focus on collecting life experiences rather than things.

- Mistakes are learning experiences; blunders are a part of professional life.

- Change is good.

---

3. I love this quote from a Wired.com interview with musician Herbie Hancock (www .herbiehancock.com): "I have not shut myself off from learning, and the value and beauty of learning and expanding, exploring. That gets my adrenaline going. But I had the great advantage of working with Miles Davis back in the '60s, who encouraged his young musicians (I was young then) to explore, to take chances, to go outside the box. And I've never forgotten those lessons" (van Buskirk, 2007).

Beliefs That Enhance Hipness

- Leadership changes with the situation.

- Young professionals are interested in learning from me.

- I have a responsibility—a duty—to mentor younger professionals.

- Technology is my friend. I should learn about the technologies that younger professionals are using to communicate and connect at work.

- I need to initiate and build relationships with younger workers. Leadership is social—with every conversation I can make a situation better or worse.

- Young professionals might have different beliefs about work. They see things differently. I should not expect them to think and act the way I think and act.

- It is my responsibility to be open and responsive to new ideas and approaches. I will be more successful and work will be more enjoyable if I am flexible.

- Talent comes in many packages. I can admire the talent and be a fan of someone half my age who talks, dresses, and acts in ways that seem strange to me.

podcasts and can name several of their favorite bloggers. The fifty-year-olds have written off e-mail as a tool for the young.

The preceding lists of hip and sage beliefs make a starter set for you to consider including as part of your definition of success. Beliefs are powerful; when you take on a new belief, you see new possibilities, choose new actions, and produce new results.

A Story About Time

Sometimes we believe something—with all our might—but we don't understand what the belief really means. I worked with a large organization that had about six hundred middle managers. The senior management team hired me to help them realign the middle management function because their managers were leaving and fewer people were applying for open positions.

I asked the senior management team about their values, goals, and priorities. They mentioned many times that they felt that a manager's time was precious. They told me they believed time was a precious resource.

I interviewed many middle managers and met with the senior management team several times. I wrote a report of my findings and recommendations. I presented my findings to the full senior management team. One of my observations was that senior managers did not value time. As you might imagine, this assertion drew strong negative reactions from the senior management team, who were convinced that they did value time. I then listed the reasons I had come to this conclusion:

- Middle managers were bogged down by hundreds of e-mails that required no action and provided no worth-while information.

- In the name of inclusion, middle managers were as-signed to multiple committees, sometimes as many as six at a time. Each of these committees had multiple meetings.

- The number of reports that middle managers were being asked to complete was rising.

- The performance evaluation forms were twenty-five pages long and the average middle manager had fifty direct reports to evaluate.

- The organization had recently implemented new time-keeping and recruiting systems that required more time than the old ones to use.

These are just a few of the observations, but what I was seeing was that the middle managers' time was treated as though it were a cheap and renewable resource—not precious and finite. The senior team sat in silence as I shared my observations, and slowly they saw that they did not value time.

Sometimes we say we believe something but do not think through what this really means. If you value time, then you should make decisions that do not waste it.[4]

Imagine the possibilities, actions, and results that would pour from a mind-set that included these beliefs. POW! What a powerful definition of success! Imagine what an organization would look and feel like if all professionals over forty held these beliefs. The atmosphere would be electric, exciting, and highly productive.

You can adopt these beliefs right now, and they will begin to work for you immediately. You will notice different things and seek different conversations and choose different courses of

---

4. I admit that the notion of valuing time is a bit of a hot button for me because I see so much time frittered away. We are bcc'd and cc'd and reply-all'd way too much. If this topic interests you, you may enjoy a popular post on Management Craft called "The Cost of Communication Is Too High Most of the Time." You can find it here: http://managementcraft.typepad.com/management_craft/2007/03/the_cost_of_com.html.

action. Your definition of success acts as a filter. Ideally, you want to define success in ways that support your goals and priorities. If you want to be hip and sage, the beliefs listed in the box will serve you well.

I have given many presentations and taught classes about designing our definition of success, and I find that some people struggle with the concept of taking on a new belief. They ask me how they can just start believing something they did not believe the day before. They think that beliefs happen over time and naturally. Many long-held beliefs do come from years of observation and experiences. We adopt new beliefs in an instant, too. Have you ever thought, "I would not have believed it had I not seen it with my own eyes?" Can you recall a time when you met someone who made a poor first impression but who later became a close friend? Have you ever changed your mind about an issue after watching an exposé on *60 Minutes*? We discard and take on new beliefs all the time.

A second question I get asked a lot is how—as in what process to use—do I adopt a belief? This is a great question because we often make the process more difficult than it should be. The Beliefs–Actions–Results Cycle is self-reinforcing—beliefs lead to actions that produce results that reinforce or change beliefs. The process of adopting new beliefs, then, should focus on behaving your way through the Beliefs–Actions–Results Cycle. To institutionalize the hip and sage beliefs, try the following:

- Review the hip and sage beliefs daily to keep them top of mind.

- When creating and reviewing your to-do or project list, ask yourself if the listed tasks reflect your interest in being hip and sage.

- Focus on learning one new method or how to use one new tool each month.

- Change your context so that it reinforces your new beliefs (the Tony-Bennett-plays-MTV method).

- Do something every day that enables you to communicate, connect, and collaborate with younger professionals.

- Carve away the barriers and diversions that do not support your goals and priorities.

BELIEFS THAT NO LONGER SERVE YOU

In addition to adopting new beliefs that support your goals, you may need to discard old beliefs that are not useful or are not serving you well. How do you know if your definition of success is constructive? The following questions can help you diagnose whether your current beliefs are helpful or harmful:

- Are you happy? Are you satisfied with the contribution you are making at work? Do you feel relevant? If not, why not? What beliefs might be responsible for this shortfall?

- Identify the changes you resist. Why are you resisting? What do you believe about the change that is holding you back?

- Think about how you feel as an older professional within your organization. What are you telling yourself about what it means to be older than most of your colleagues?

A belief does not have to be wrong for you to consider abandoning it. Many perfectly valid and logical beliefs get in the way. For example, you might believe that the young engineers in your department don't want to listen to your old-fogie ideas. And the young engineers might indeed avoid asking you for your ideas. Your belief is backed up by valid observations—but does that make it helpful? No. You would be better served by adopting a new belief and discarding this old-fogie one. For example, your goals would be better served if you chose to believe that you can communicate and connect with young engineers by showing more interest in and respect for their talents. Taking on this belief would lead to a different set of actions and a different mind-set—you would generate a new vibe that the engineers would surely notice.

Nonproductive beliefs are behind many of our disappointments. If a project did not go well, do a postmortem to discover why this was the case and to understand the thinking that allowed the failure to occur. Was it bad assumptions? Fuzzy expectations due to inadequate communication? If you could do things over, which actions or decisions would you change? What are the beliefs and assumptions that drove these actions? Abandoning beliefs that do not serve your goals and priorities is just as important as taking on the hip and sage definition of success.

YOUR OWN BELIEFS AND DEFINITION OF SUCCESS

In addition to, or instead of, using the hip and sage definition of success, you can easily define the set of beliefs that will best serve your goals and priorities by completing Worksheet 2:

1. In column A, list the goals that you most want to achieve
   in the next year or two. If you have a longer-term goal, that
   is fine too, but define which part of that goal you want to
   accomplish in the next year.

2. For each of these goals, identify in column B one or two
   beliefs that would support your success. What mind-set is
   going to best facilitate goal attainment?

3. In column C, identify an action consistent with these beliefs
   that you will complete in the next month.

4. In column D, identify an action consistent with these beliefs
   that you will complete in the next week.

5. Review your worksheet daily, making adjustments to fine-
   tune your goals, beliefs, and actions. Complete the actions.

6. Take thirty minutes to repeat this exercise every month.
   If you do this, you will get better results.

WORKSHEET 2 **YOUR BELIEFS AND DEFINITION OF SUCCESS**

A. GOALS	B. BELIEFS	C. MONTHLY ACTIONS	D. WEEKLY ACTIONS

CHANGING BELIEFS AND REDEFINING SUCCESS

While some beliefs are easy to identify, we may not know or acknowledge what we believe until we explore our definition of success. Beliefs can last a lifetime or change in an instant. We are in charge when it comes to beliefs, and we can choose, take on, and discard beliefs at any time, just a we can redefine success for ourselves.

8

Job Seeking and Hiring for the Hip and Sage

You've explored your own sageness, learned how to become and stay hip, and defined your success—but what about your job? I have heard from many older job seekers that it is a struggle to land a great job. Younger people vying for the same positions will often work for less money and bring in more up-to-date skills. I don't want to brush this concern under the rug by suggesting that with the right outfit and training you can level the playing field. I think it will be harder for a fifty-something to land many jobs when competing against a thirty-something with similar skills.

If you're on the hiring side, remember that hiring the best-qualified candidate for a position does not necessarily mean hiring the most experienced. If a job calls for someone with ten years' experience in marketing, having twenty years' experience may not make a difference. A candidate with ten years' experience might be the most qualified given other factors.

Throughout my career, I have hired a lot of people and interviewed many smart people who did not get a job offer. I do leadership recruiting as a consultant and I have been an HR leader within several companies. In this chapter, I offer fifteen tips that will help you be a more competitive job candidate, followed by five tips for hip and sage professionals who are hiring younger professionals.

FIFTEEN WAYS TO IMPROVE YOUR ODDS OF LANDING A GREAT JOB

There are three times in the life cycle of a job search that I think make a big difference. The first starts well before you begin looking for a job. The second starts when you begin looking for a job in earnest, and the third is the job interview itself.

BEFORE THE JOB SEARCH

Search Tip #1: Get hip.

In his best-selling book *Never Eat Alone* (2005), author Keith Ferrazzi suggests that we build it before we need it.[1] The "it" he is talking about is our network. A lot of people start building a network after they have been laid off or decide they want a career change, and this is way too late. I think the same can be said of having our skills up-to-date. It's best to be ready and qualified well before we decide to change jobs. Establish connections with younger professionals and learn about the new technologies. The hip and sage will have a strategic advantage over sage professionals who have not taken the time to improve their hipness.

In particular, I recommend that you understand the following technologies well enough to converse about them in an interview:

---

1. You can find the Never Eat Alone blog here: http://nevereatalone.typepad.com.

- Web meetings

- Blogs

- Podcasting

- BlackBerrys

- Wikis

- Social networking

- Viral marketing

DURING THE JOB SEARCH

Search Tip #2: Be where they are.

This tip is the most important. Remember the Tony-Bennett-plays-MTV method of juxtaposition from chapter 6? Apply it to your job search and be where the people who hire are. Time is precious, so you do not need to go overboard by joining every organization under the sun. Join one organization, and become a volunteer for that organization to meet more people. Go to all the monthly meetings and connect with people. Read the top five blogs for the industry and subscribe to one or two podcasts. Attend the most important conference of the year and take lots of your business cards to the conference—and bring none of them home with you. If you have more than one conference or organization from which to choose, select the one that most attracts younger professionals.

Search Tip #3: Circumvent the application process.

I don't think you will get much agreement on this next tip from human resources professionals. Do it anyway! People who play by the rules do not stand out, and this is doubly so regarding the application process. If you are dutifully sending in your applications using those online application programs that many large companies use, you are going to need a lot of luck to get noticed. I am not suggesting that you do anything outrageous, like becoming a stalker or sending roses to the recruiter (I prefer chocolate), but I do have a few suggestions that are tame enough that they will not hurt your chances of landing an interview:

- If you have to use the online application tool, supplement this with a mailed résumé and an e-mailed résumé. If the e-mail address for the HR department is not published, a safe guess is jobs@_____.com.

- Call the human resources department. It does not hurt to call once. Keep calling and your application will be ignored. All I recommend saying during this call is that you are very interested in the position, meet the qualifications, and have done some research on the company, and you think it could be a great fit. Finish by saying that you would love to schedule an interview and have some flexibility this week and next.

- Scour your network for someone who works at the company or knows someone who does. Ask for an informal coffee chat about the company and position.

Search Tip #4: Create an online résumé or blog.

Recruiters are using the Web to find and check out candidates. Give them something to find! Create a blog that offers provocative and evocative posts and that shows off your skills and experiences. If you are a fifty-something with a great blog, this will serve you well. Make sure you do not post anything that might be embarrassing or turn an employer off. I favor having a blog, but if you do not want to commit to posting regularly, have a static site (updated often) with your bio, résumé, and stories about your career experiences. Don't include a picture unless you think this is an asset.[2] Put the URL for your site at the top of your résumé, along with your address, phone number, and e-mail address. Put your blog address in your e-mail signature as well.

Search Tip #5: Ask young colleagues at other companies to broker introductions.

If you can get someone from within the company to introduce you and your résumé to the hiring manager and recruiter, your résumé will go to the top of the pile. While you will take any introduction you can get, it is better if the introduction comes from a younger professional because this will help neutralize concerns about age and hipness. If thirty-something Susan forwards your résumé, the recruiter will tend to think about you as the same mental age as Susan.

Search Tip #6: Create a hip résumé.

You are your résumé. Is your résumé hip? Remember what our definition of hip means—communicating, connecting, and collaborating with younger professionals. A hip résumé goes beyond listing job titles and dates to tell stories about your experiences. Highlight accomplishments by describing the contributions you have made in your various jobs. How did you

---

2. My agent once told me that I should not ask the publisher to put my picture on the cover of my book unless I looked like a supermodel. I understand what he was saying—for better or worse, we judge people based on looks.

improve the business? Here are a couple of other practical ré-sumé-writing tips for the hip and sage:

- Keep your résumé to two or three pages. You can share fewer details for jobs you held more than fifteen years ago.

- Never share your age, and offer dates only when necessary. You do not need to share the year you graduated from college or high school on your résumé.

- Emphasize your knowledge and skills, especially those relating to new technologies and methods.

Search Tip #7: Structure your life to meet your career goals.

What do you want to be when you grow up? Your next career may require that you make a few lifestyle changes. Will you need to travel or work odd hours? How much will this job pay? Salaries are usually based on market rates for the job, not the experience of the holder, although there is usually a range within the job grade. I have worked with several older professionals who believed that they deserved to be paid at least as much as they made at previous positions. If the job they are applying for is different from the prior one, the conclusion does not make sense. A friend of mine told me that he was worth $200,000 and that he would not work for less. While I wish him well, I think this is an unproductive way to navigate the job market. You are not worth X dollars; the job pays Y dollars. If you decide to change careers, you might need to adjust your lifestyle to live off a lower salary (or a higher one). Think about and make these adjustments before you seek new work. Determine the type of work you want to do, then think salary. If you consider only jobs that pay X dollars or more, you might pass up an opportunity to find a great job.

IN THE JOB INTERVIEW

Search Tip #8: Look good.

Hip and sage professionals need to look great at interviews. If your wardrobe is out-of-date, buy a new outfit. Mind the details by ensuring that your shoes and accessories are all stylish. Hairstyle and complexion are important, too—be sure you don't look like yesterday's middle manager. This is an important tip for being a hip and sage professional even if you are not looking for a new job. If you are not sure what to wear, ask for help. Get your clothes and haircuts at places where younger professionals shop—not Grampa's barbershop.

Search Tip #9: Be prepared.

I get turned off in an interview if it is clear to me that the candidate did not take the time to do a little research. With all the information available on the Internet, there is no excuse for not being prepared. I want to know that you have thoroughly read the company's Web site and learned about our business. I would also recommend that you do a Google search on the hiring manager and the human resources person with whom you will be meeting.[3]

---

3. Doing a Google search on someone means putting his or her name in the Google search engine and seeing what comes up. To narrow your results, put the name in quotes, like this: "Lisa Haneberg." It is a good idea to search on your own name to see what comes up. I often search on the names of candidates—don't you want to know what I am going to find out about you?

Search Tip #10: Ask great questions.

An interview is a two-way conversation and a two-sided exploration. So take advantage of it and ask great questions. I reject candidates who do not ask great questions because they are not doing their part to determine if the job and company are a good fit for them. I expect people to ask tough questions. I want candidates to be interested enough in the job to take the interview process seriously. Great questions are open-ended questions about business goals, the organization's culture, and the expectations that will be placed on the person taking the job.[4]

Search Tip #11: Be open and relaxed.

Although an interview is a formal discussion, you do not want to come across as a stiff. Take the interview questions seriously but talk in a casual tone—more like what you would do at a networking event. While we all get nervous at job interviews, hip and sage professionals need to overcompensate to ensure that we do not come across as stodgy or rigid. Short of knocking back a few shots of whiskey (which would be bad), do whatever it takes to be relaxed. When we are nervous, we tighten up and our listening skills plummet. This is a problem because you want to make sure you hear and understand all the questions you are being asked. I once interviewed a guy who was so nervous, he answered most of the questions with responses that did not address my questions. I felt for the guy and had him come back a second time—when he did much better. But interviewees don't usually get a second chance. Don't buy one of those books

---

4. My most popular blog post on Management Craft—by far—was a post I did in 2005 called "How to Interview Potential Employers." You can read the post here: http://managementcraft.typepad.com/management_craft/2005/03/how_to_intervie.html.

with interview questions, either—there is nothing worse than sitting across the desk from someone who has obviously practiced their answers. Remember transparency! I want candidates to answer fully and from their hearts and brains—no practice needed.

Search Tip #12: Be likable.

For each job, there may be several candidates who have the basic qualifications. With more than one good candidate, who gets the job? The person who gets the job is the one that the interviewers liked the most. Likability is critical—*critical*. Likability is perhaps the most important thing during the interview. Sure, you need to be able to do the functions of the job, but beyond this hiring managers want to believe that they will enjoy working with you. Hip and sage professionals need to show their personalities. But if your best friend has told you that you sound grouchy when you talk (even if you are not), you have a challenge to overcome. No one will hire a grouchy candidate. I was interviewing a fifty-something woman a month ago. She was a lovely woman, but she came across as sarcastic and negative. The hiring manager was a thirty-something, and this woman immediately put her off because she was imagining what it would be like to work with her every day.

Search Tip #13: Flash your iPhone.

You are hip and sage. You look good and your résumé sings. Why not add a little bling? Go ahead and flash your iPhone. I remember the week I got my Kindle. The Kindle was on back-order and only those folks who ordered the day it launched were getting one from the first shipment. Everywhere I went—the airport, the coffee shop, the office, people were drawn to my Kindle. When the iPhone came out it attracted the same kind of attention. If you think you will be competing for this position against younger professionals, why not stage a little peek at your iPhone or BlackBerry. A recruiter or hiring manager who sees that you have an iPhone will know that you are hip.

Search Tip #14: Remember names.

We are self-absorbed beasts and love it when people remember who we are. Write down the names of the people you are meeting with at the top of your pad of paper. Work in their names during the conversation. Something like this:

> *Lisa, that is a great question. While at Black & Decker, I created a cross-functional project team to . . .*

Don't go overboard—just use the interviewer's name two or three times during an hour-long interview.

Search Tip #15: Ask for the job.

I want to hire someone who really wants the job. This might seem obvious, but interest and passion levels vary a great deal among candidates. Some people are interviewing for the job because they need a job and not necessarily because they are drawn to this job. I want to know that a candidate will pour his or her heart into the work. I recommend that you close the interview by letting the interviewer know that you are very interested in the job. Tell the interviewer why the job interests you and show a little passion for it.

These fifteen tips will help you be a more competitive job candidate. Hip and sage professionals know that communication, connection, and collaboration are important elements of strong business relationships. A job interview offers you the opportunity to start building a relationship that could last years. Interviewers hire candidates with whom they connect.

FIVE TIPS FOR HIP AND SAGE HIRING MANAGERS

Hiring decisions are among the most important you will ever make at work. It is tough to select from a pool of qualified candidates based on one or two conversations. Biases and personal preferences get in the way and make the decision more subjective—and the decision is bound to be subjective, no matter how much you try to keep things logical. The following tips assume that you know how to evaluate a candidate's basic qualifications. The next challenge is to determine which person is a better fit for the job, the team, and the organization.

Hiring Tip #1: Hire to fill skill gaps.

Many hiring managers hire in their own image, leaving the department looking and feeling very homogeneous. It is better to do the opposite—hire people who have strengths where your skills are weak. Think about the strengths of the various members of your team. Hire the candidate that will best round out the team's strengths.

Hiring Tip #2: Hire for passion.

Once you have determined that a candidate has the basic skills and experiences to do the job, look for some of the more intangible qualities. It's better to hire someone who is marginally qualified but very passionate about the industry and work than a highly qualified person who does not seem emotionally connected to the work. When you look for passion, do not simply focus on extroversion. Even reflective introverts can show passion for the work through their descriptions and responses during the interview. I remember a situation where we were hiring a department director and had gotten down to two candidates. One candidate—who was older, by the way—had much more experience. The younger candidate had less experience but much more enthusiasm. We hired the younger candidate and never regretted it. Had the older candidate showed the same level of passion for the work, he would have been hired in an instant—but he didn't.

Hiring Tip #3: Hire for excellence.

Every hiring and promotion decision we make communicates our definition of excellence to the organization. When you bring in new employees, you are essentially saying, *This is what I want from employees.* Every new hire ought to reinforce your definition of excellence in terms of skills, quality of work, and team relationships. Your reputation is on the line with each hire you make.

Hiring Tip #4: Relax your personal style standards.

Younger professionals may see things differently than we do. As a candidate, you want to look good. As an interviewer, you don't want to get hung up on looks and style. If we allow ourselves to pass judgment on people because of the way they dress or look, we may miss seeing their amazing talents. What would you do if a job candidate came to an interview dressed in casual clothes and sporting a lip ring? Do nothing. Most younger workers will know to look their best for a job interview, but some style choices, like body piercings, tattoos, and strange haircuts, might be hard to hide.

Hiring Tip #5: Apply the Tony Bennett approach test.

When you are hiring new employees, consider whether you can learn from them. Is this candidate someone who will push you and help you grow? Might this candidate be someone you can develop to take your role one day? Your legacy as a leader shows up in your employees.

The bottom line is that we need to focus on talent, not the package it comes in. Hire professionals who can mentor you on the latest technologies and those who seem interested in and eager to learn from you. Notice any judgments you make about candidates and check to make sure these judgments will serve your goal of building a great team.

The Hip & Sage You

Authors are often asked what difference they hope their work will make. My goals for this book are perhaps the highest I've ever had: I would like *Hip & Sage* to catalyze a revolution. There is nothing so powerful and transformative as a strong partnership and collaboration between our sages and our youths.

In the first part of the book, I offer a model for sageness. After reading the "Sage" section, I hope you have a deeper understanding of your sageness and a greater appreciation for the process we all go through to become refined creatures. Your sageness is how your strengths, style, and experiences turn goals into reality. You are a sage.

Then in "Hip" I suggest a new definition of hipness—one that focuses on how we communicate, connect, and collaborate with younger professionals. I prefer this definition to others that stress the importance of Prada handbags, Armani suits, and Jimmy Choo shoes. And while relationships are what we strive to create, sometimes the pathway to hipness goes through new technologies. Younger professionals communicate with their friends in ways that may seem strange to us. To communicate, connect, and collaborate, we might also need to IM, blog, and podcast. I hope "New Technologies 101" piques your interest, gives you a few new ideas, and provides a good base of awareness for several popular tech tools.

In the third section of the book, "Hip & Sage," I bring the concepts of sageness and hipness together and emphasize the importance of how we define success. It might be that all you need to do is shift your mind-set—just a tad—to experience a breakthrough in hipness.

I am inspired by people who embrace learning and reinvention with gusto. Here is an exuberant quote from William Shatner (remember *Star Trek*?) in a January 2008 *Details* magazine article:[1]

Life motivates me. Ideas motivate me. I want to do a talk show. I have ideas for three animated films. I'm nearly finished with my autobiography. I continue to write Star Trek–*themed novels. My daughter and I have extremely successful Web sites and a video blog, even though my computer's still in the box it arrived in. As long as my body holds up, my mind is as willing as it's ever been.* (Hochman, 2008)

Shatner has revitalized his career and is as popular today as he was as a young lad playing Captain Kirk. *Revitalize, reinvent, re-create, recover.* "Re" implies change, and change gets harder and harder as we mature. We get set in our ways and comfortable with the ways we have learned to get things done. One of the greatest challenges for the hip and sage is to embrace change and learn how to live nimbly. Here is another excellent quote from my conversation with Susan Ayers Walker:

As you get older it's harder and harder to change, and in order to be hip you've got to be able to accept change. You've

---

1. The *Details* article is titled "Wiseguy: William Shatner" and it was written by David Hochman. Find the article here: http://men.style.com/details/features/full?id=content_6267.

got to be able to understand that there's opportunity in change and that change is a good thing and change is not going to stop. And the problem with getting older is that it's harder and harder to be accepting of change and that's why young people tend to look at old people as irrelevant and that's why older people get pushed out of organizations —because they're not willing to change. They're not willing to roll with the punches. It drives me crazy when I hear older workers say that this is not the way they used to do things. Well, I'm sorry, but we used to write on a typewriter. Now we use computers. The next step is that we're all going to be texting instead of calling. In order to be hip you have to understand change and be strong enough to decide whether you want to go along with the change.

Nimbleness, like hipness, is fueled with a powerful mindset. Change will come more easily if we take on the beliefs that serve our goals. Here are a few beliefs I have adopted to improve my receptivity to change:

- I want my work to be useful and well received. If I need to adjust my methods to reach more people and help others access my work, then this is a small price to pay.

- My career goals will be well served if I role-model flexibility and nimbleness.

- How something is accomplished matters far less than the impact it has on others.

- I know I am learning when I feel like I am out of my comfort zone, just as I know I'm getting stronger when my muscles are sore after a three-mile hike.

When I think of what it looks like and feels like to be hip and sage, two words come to mind—*vigor* and *regeneration*. Vigor is strength and health—our sageness is our power. Regeneration is the process of creating life. Hipness is how we breathe new life into our careers and the careers of the young professionals we affect.

Resources

A Glossary of Hip

2People: A *social networking* site for people interested in environmental sustainability.

AARP Groups: Online communities hosted on the AARP Web site, listed by area of interest.

Acrobat Connect Professional/Personal Web Conferencing: A Web conferences provider for businesses and individuals.

aggregator: A program or application that collects, or aggregates, online content delivered through *RSS feeds* (*blogs,* news Web sites, *social networking* feeds).

Apple: The company that makes Macintosh computers, iPods, iPhones, and other hip gadgets.

Audacity: A free open-source program for recording and editing audio files.

blog: See *weblog.*

blogosphere: A term used by bloggers to describe the collective world of *blogs.*

Carnival of the Capitalists: A weekly collection of business *blog* posts hosted by a different blogger each week.

CycleSpace: A *social networking* site for motorcycle enthusiasts.

Dynametric: The company that makes a simple device that connects your phone to your computer for recording *podcast* interviews.

Eons: A *social networking* site for Baby Boomers.

Facebook: A popular *social networking* site.

Fifty fun things to do with your iPod: A Web site that offers ideas for ways to use an *iPod* device. (Most of the ideas would also apply to other MP3 players.)

Flickr: A Web site where people load and share photos.

Go To Meeting: A popular Web meeting and *webinar* service provider.

Great Web Meetings: A company that teaches professionals how to deliver great Web-based meetings and presentations.

Hipcast: A Web-based hosting service for *podcasts* and videocasts.

hipness: The ability to communicate, connect, and collaborate with younger generations. In business, your hipness determines how effectively you work with, inspire, and influence younger workers. Hip entrepreneurs are able to enroll, engage, and excite younger customers and business partners.

HTML code: Statements in HyperText Markup Language, the predominant language for coding Web pages and *blog* posts.

IM: Instant messaging, better known as IM or IMing in Internet slang; allows you to send real-time messages to individuals on your buddy or contact list. You type messages into a small window that shows up on your screen and your buddy's screen, like a typed telephone call.

iPod: A small, handheld media center with a digital audio player, video player, photo viewer, and portable hard drive, made by Apple.

link love: A term bloggers use to describe when one blogger writes about and links to another. To get link love, you must first give lots and lots of link love.

LinkedIn: A popular *social networking* site.

Live Meeting: A popular Web meeting and *webinar* service provider.

MySpace: A popular *social networking* site.

permalink: A URL (Web address) that points to a specific *blog* post.

plogging: Maintaining a graphic *weblog.*

podcast: An audio segment delivered via *RSS feed* to *iPods* and other portable media players. To podcast is to create, upload, and distribute podcast episodes.

Podcast Alley: A Web portal where you can find and subscribe to *podcasts.*

PodcastBunker: A Web portal where you can find and subscribe to *podcasts.*

Podcasting Tools: A Web site that offers tutorials and informational articles about podcasting.

ProvoEvo: A conjunction of the words *provocative* and *evocative.* To engage, excite, and enroll employees and customers, our stories and conversations must be both evocative and provocative.

Really Simple Syndication (RSS): A format for notifying users when content has been updated on a subscribed list of Web sites, *blogs,* and *podcasts.*

RSS feed: How you receive an RSS document, which is called a feed or channel, and which contains either a summary of content from an associated Web site or the full text. An RSS aggregator, or reader, automatically checks your subscribed feeds regularly for content and downloads updates to your computer or mobile device.

sageness: Your natural strengths and characteristics, goals and priorities, and experiences—manifested as skills, drive, judgment, and knowledge—that have been honed, carved, seasoned, and polished through the years. Your sageness is unique; it may or may not be visible to others or in use contributing to the world.

search engine optimization (SEO): The process of increasing desirable traffic to a Web site.

Second Life: A virtual world. I know several professionals who have set up virtual meeting rooms in their virtual worlds. Their avatars meet to discuss real business problems and then tell their human equivalents what was decided.

Skype: One of the most popular *VoIP* providers; it lets you make free calls over the Internet to anyone else who also has the service.

social networking: A term used to describe participation in online communities and online relationship building.

streaming video: Video that can be played from a Web site by using a streaming provider—a program or service provider that acts as the video player.

TeeBeeDee: A popular *social networking* site targeted to people over forty years of age.

text message: A short typed message sent by or to mobile phones and personal digital assistants. In text messages, words are often abbreviated to keep the message within the device's character limit (often 160 characters or less).

ThirdAge: A Web portal targeted to readers age forty and older.

trackback: A URL (web address) for a specific *blog* post that links back to the original post and lets the post author know that his or her post was referenced by another blogger or Web site author.

Twitter: An online service that allows users to create communities and share their lives. Twittering involves a combination of *blogs, IM,* and the cell phone. People post about what they are doing—mowing the grass, reading blogs, painting toenails.

unconference: A participant-driven conference that often includes a higher level of participation and flexibility and is designed to look and feel very different from traditional conferences. Generally does not have high-priced keynote presenters, high registration fees, or detailed schedules.

viral: Refers to viral marketing, or techniques that increase product or brand awareness by word-of-mouth communication or its online equivalents.

vlogging: Video *podcasting.*

VoIP: Voice-over-Internet protocol; used for Internet telephony (with companies such as *Skype* or Vonage).

webcast: See *webinar.*

WebEx: A popular Web meeting and *webinar* service provider.

webinar: Refers to Web conferencing or Web meetings; a seminar on the Web is a webinar. Webinars allow you to conduct live sales meetings, presentations, seminars, and ad hoc meetings over the Internet.

weblog (blog): A Web site with specialized software to make adding and updating content quick and easy (many bloggers update their blog on a daily basis). Blogs are often described as online journals featuring news articles and links to other blogs. Most experienced bloggers agree that in order to be a true blog, it must be published to an RSS feed.

Wet Paint: An online company that offers a network of free *wiki* sites.

wiki: An open, collaborative Web site where users and contributors can add, remove, and edit content using a Web browser.

Wikipedia: A free online encyclopedia built using *wiki* software.

Wikispaces: A company that provides free *wikis.*

Woot: A Web site that liquidates tech products at low prices; but you have to be fast and check often to get in on the limited quantities.

Yahoo Groups: A service provided by Yahoo that allows people to create their own e-mail or Web-driven group discussion areas.

YouTube: An online source where you can find video clips on most topics and interests—uploaded by millions of global users.

Zune: An MP3 player made by Microsoft.

A Primer on
the Generations

For the first time in our history, we have four generations working together as employees—or trying to work together. Many differences among these generations make the challenge of building and maintaining relationships especially difficult. This quote from *Boomers, Xers, and Other Strangers* states it well:

> *The differences between generations are more than just distinct ways of looking at things or new solutions for problems. They're gut-level differences in values that involve a person's beliefs, emotions, and preferences.* (Hicks and Hicks, 1999, p. 4)

Here's how companies, and you as a hip and sage professional, can appeal to all generations:

- Examine the background and characteristics of each generation to understand the unique talents, challenges, and emerging trends it offers that benefit all generations. For instance, most workers today are asking for flexible work environments so they can take care of their family (elderly parents as well as children), pursue higher education, or work part-time. Regardless of generation, we all appreciate an employer that allows us the freedom to balance our personal and professional lives.

- Delve into the motivators of each generation, and use this information to hone your communications and workflow

- Tailor your managerial approach and encourage the organization to craft roles, compensation, and benefits targeted at the needs of each group

Following is an overview of the generations and their characteristics.

TRADITIONALISTS (BORN 1900–1945)

Traditionalists are employees over sixty-three. Many of them were born before World War II and have memories of growing up during the Great Depression. They define a typical work environment as one where individuals work in the office from 8 a.m. to 5 p.m. Many of them have retired (only approximately 5 percent of Traditionalists are in the workforce today); those that remain working are in high-level positions, well connected, and very influential.

Traditionalists:

- Are strongly influenced by family and religion

- View education as a dream and leisure time as a reward for working hard, long hours

- Feel discomfort regarding change and are uncomfortable with the ambiguity the current business environment offers

- Trust authority, respect rules, and are hardworking

- Are loyal to their employers and spend most of their career working for one or two companies

- Put work before pleasure

- Expect people to "pay their dues" before being given authority

- Place great value on financial security

- Come from a generation in which most husbands worked long hours at the office while their nonworking wives handled household and family matters

Some important things to consider as you strive to motivate and meet the needs of these workers:

- Younger managers should acknowledge the expertise and knowledge that older workers bring to the workplace; these workers can be great resources, particularly when it comes to company and customer history.

- Don't assume that older workers aren't technologically adept or can't become so. Many, in fact, are quite tech-savvy and enjoy the challenges that come with mastering new skills.

- Eliminate the age bias that often exists in hiring and development processes, and craft roles that build on the expertise of older workers.

- Make recruiting and retaining older workers for both entry-level and highly skilled work a goal for your organization.

BABY BOOMERS
(BORN 1946–1964)

Baby Boomers make up the midforties to sixty-year-old work-force. Because Traditionalists ahead of them are retiring later and the Gen Xers and Millennials are not ready to step into their positions, Baby Boomers may find that they are working longer than their Traditionalist parents did.

Baby Boomers:

- Value personal growth, hard work, individuality, and equality of the sexes

- Are ambitious, flexible, productive, self-sufficient, and people oriented

- Distrust leadership, are juggling busy lives, and demand merit-based systems and participative management

- Question authority and have led a trend toward less hierarchical work structures

- Represent the heart of today's management

- Were the first to experience having both spouses working, as well as the first to have women and men working to-gether and sharing the same responsibilities

- Had smaller families and enjoyed affluent lifestyles that led to them being labeled the "Me" generation

- May have the added burden of taking care of a parent in addition to their day job

- Are leading a trend toward delayed retirement, choosing to work at least part-time

Some important things to consider as you strive to motivate and meet the needs of these workers:

- Make their work fulfilling to them, and they will do whatever it takes to achieve the company's goals. If they don't believe in an initiative, they will disengage and stagnate, which will reduce productivity and company morale.

- Giving them new assignments and placing them in mentoring and knowledge-sharing roles or even career moves within the organization can reengage them. Mentoring allows them to enjoy new challenges while also ensuring their institutional knowledge is transferred to newer employees.

- Examine compensation and benefit policies to ensure these employees are not penalized financially just because their company needs them to stay at a certain level.

GENERATION XERS
(BORN 1965–1980)

There are fewer Gen Xers than Baby Boomers. What they learned from their Baby Boom parents is the toll it can take on a family when both parents are working and trying to "have it all." Their desire to change this dynamic is what created the trend toward work–life balance and changed the definition of company loyalty. Most value their families more highly than their work, which means they are less likely to work for one employer, as they will go to the company that best fits their needs.

Gen Xers:

- See change as the rule rather than the exception

- Are technologically savvy and pragmatic

- Think globally

- Are self-reliant, optimistic, confident, and unimpressed by authority

- Value education, independence, diversity, and parenting more than they value their work

- Dislike authority and rigid work requirements

- Want to do it their way and just get it done—they want the freedom to work on projects that suit them wherever is more convenient; cubicles stifle their development

- Have a greater commitment to their work, their team, and their immediate boss than to the company

- Seek balance in their life as they raise their family

- Tend to be more family oriented than Baby Boomers

- Desire a fun workplace

Some important things to consider as you strive to motivate and meet the needs of these workers:

- Give them the flexibility to work when and where they want to work.

- Understand that Gen Xers take their careers seriously—but rather than climbing the ladder, as was the norm among earlier generations, they see their career as more fluid. This means they often move laterally or stop and start working depending on personal or family needs.

- Provide them with immediate and ongoing feedback on their performance as this encourages them to find new and more effective ways to improve processes or execute tasks.

- Provide guidance in a hands-off way, meaning you should not provide step-by-step directions. They need freedom to create and produce.

- Recognize that they are comfortable sharing feedback with others, and it is important to solicit their feedback on an ongoing basis to try to retain them. If Gen Xers are not satisfied with their job, they will not waste time complaining. Instead, they will send out résumés and accept the best offer available.

- Motivate them by giving them opportunities to learn new skills. They are motivated by enhancing their skill set because they want to continue to grow their worth so they are even more employable.

MILLENNIALS
(BORN 1981–1999)

The workers in this new generation are in their twenties and are called Millennials, the Internet generation, or Generation Y.

They are sometimes also called Echo Boomers, because they are the largest generation since the Baby Boomers. They expect to assume a high level of responsibility and to have their feedback welcomed immediately upon beginning a job. This is different from the attitude of generations before them, who expected people to demonstrate their ability to take on more responsibility and earn their way to the top.

Millennials:

- Offer multitasking, goal-setting, and social networking skills

- Value a flexible working environment and have taken work–life balance a step further even than Gen Xers

- Want open spaces, lower walls, and the freedom to leave the office—or at least the feeling that the office is a place where they're free to move around

- Want jobs with flexibility, including telecommuting options and the ability to work part-time or to leave the workforce temporarily when having children

- Were exposed to diverse lifestyles and cultures in school at an early age, and tend to respect different races, ethnic groups, and sexual orientations

- Are accustomed to computer technology, immediacy, and multitasking

- Have short attention spans—hence the multitasking

- Are inclined to be less loyal to an employer than their predecessors were, and more likely to change jobs frequently

- Have no fear when it comes to making decisions quickly

- Value professional development and strive to work faster and better

- Want creative challenges and projects with deadlines so that they can own their tasks

- Regard their relationship with their immediate managers as having greater value than the relationship they have with the company

- Want their employer to treat them as if they are customers and ask them "How are we doing? What can we do to make things better for you?"

Some important things to consider as you strive to motivate and meet the needs of these workers:

- Appeal to their need for a sense of community, greater responsibility, hands-on participation, and ongoing recognition.

- Build on their network-centric attitudes by creating a strong social fabric at work. This can be done by using many of the technologies described in this book.

- Solicit their input. They want to be a part of the process.

- Give younger workers an opportunity to serve in roles that allow them to acquire greater responsibility.

- Recognize that younger workers are likely to leave your organization for education, travel, or another job. Make it easy for them to return, if it is in the best interest of the company.

- Reward results, not face time.

Alexandra Levit is a consultant who writes and speaks about how to improve multigenerational communication and relationship building at work.[1] She is the author of *They Don't Teach Corporate in College* and several other books on jobs, hiring, and retention. I recently spoke with Alexandra about how Boomers can better manage Millennials. Here is a fascinating excerpt that basically says that we (the Boomers) caused our own management challenge!

Millennials want to work for a manager who treats them like a colleague rather than a subordinate. They want a manager who's open to giving and receiving feedback. I've had Boomers say that if they let their Millennials come into their offices all day long, they would never get any work done. Combat this by scheduling a few minutes every day to meet with your Millennials.

The worst thing you can do to a Millennial is say, "You're right, that's a problem; I'll take care of it," and then never follow through. They can't stand that. This is a generation that's not content to sit around for five years waiting for a promotion. Millennials want immediate recognition, even if it's not financial or hierarchical, and they want to be patted on the back for a job well done. The Millennials, the children of the Boomers, are the most child-centered generation in American history. Millennials are used to getting what they want quickly and being treated as though they are special. However, now that this entitled attitude has spilled out into the workplace, the Boomer bosses are singing a different tune than they did as Boomer parents. They

---

1. You can find Alexandra's blog, Water Cooler Wisdom, here: http://alexandralevit.typepad.com.

want their Millennial employees to have some deference for experience and the establishment, and to be willing to work hard.

Touché! Everyone is different and you might identify with characteristics I have listed for each of these generations. We are products of our time, however, and it is helpful for all hip and sage professionals to have a better understanding of some common traits of each generation at work.

Job Search Tips for Older Workers

Job search tips for older workers is a hot topic, and you will find lots of great articles and resources online. Here are a few:

- "Seven Job Search Tips for Older Workers," by Cynthia Ross Cowan. Published on www.50Plus.com: http://50plus .com/Employment/BrowseArticles/index.cfm?t_offset= 1&documentID=19424. Access date: August 19, 2008.

- "Eight Interview Questions for Older Workers to Antici-pate," by Shelbi Walker. Published on the AARP Bulletin, September 2002: www.aarp.org/money/work/articles/ 0905_sidebar_4.html. Access date: August 19, 2008.

- "Six Tricky Interview Questions," by Mary Quigley and Loretta Kaufman. Article published by *AARP* magazine: www.aarpmagazine.org/lifestyle/Articles/a2004-09-22- mag-interviewques.html. Access date: August 19, 2008.

- "Practical Tips for Older Workers," by Jane M. Lommel. Published by Gary Johnson's Brave New Work World and NewWork News: www.newwork.com/Pages/Networking/ 2005/Practical%20Tips.html. Access date: August 19, 2008.

- "Seven Fundamental Rules for Crafting a Rock-Solid Resume." Published by AARP Bulletin, September 2003: http://bulletin.aarp.org/yourmoney/work/articles/0905_ sidebar_3.html. Access date: August 19, 2008.

About HipandSage.com

Come visit me on HipandSage.com!

Throughout this book, I offer links to cool sites and articles. I mention blogs and podcasts and social networking sites. I suggest new technologies and offer tips for when and how to use these technologies. HipandSage.com is a portal site where you can find the live links to all these resources and many more.

- Would you like to start a blog but don't know how?

- Do you want to see a selection of social networking sites?

- Would you like to read a tutorial on how to start podcasting?

- Would you like to see my current recommendations for which blogs to put into your aggregator and which aggregator to use?

- Would you like to connect with and share ideas with other hip and sage professionals?

- Are you still wondering what twittering is all about?

You will find all this and more here—HipandSage.com is like a live version of this book. I hope to see you online.[1]

---

1. Truth be told, this Web site is more for me than for you. I have found that the best way to stay hip is to get involved. By committing to keep www.HipandSage.com provocative and evocative for hip and sage professionals, I will ensure my relevance as a writer for a few mores years! Yippee!

References and Recommended Reading

Here is a list of the sources referred to in this book, followed by a list of additional books I recommend. You can download a copy of this list with live links (where available) from www.HipandSage.com.

References

Associated Press. 2008. "Oprah Plug Makes Business Book a Hit on Web." MSNBC.com, February 17, 2008. Available online: www.msnbc.msn.com/id/23208583/. Access date: August 12, 2008.

Biography.com. N.d. Tony Bennett biography (1926–). Available online: www.biography.com/search/article.do?id=9926699. Access date: August 12, 2008.

Edelhauser, K. 2006. "Baby Boomers Starting Online Businesses in Droves." Entrepreneur.com, November 10, 2006. Available online: www.entrepreneur.com/startingabusiness/article170206.html. Access date: August 12, 2008.

Fabrikant, G. 1999. "Talking Money with Tony Bennett: His Heart's in San Francisco, His Money in His Son's Hands." *New York Times*, May 2, 1999. Available online: http://query.nytimes.com/gst/fullpage.html?res=9E01EED6113DF931A35756C0A96F958260. Access date: August 12, 2008.

Ferrazzi, K. 2005. *Never Eat Alone*. New York: Currency Doubleday.

Hicks, R., and Hicks, K. 1999. *Boomers, Xers, and Other Strangers*. Wheaton, IL: Tyndale House.

Hochman, D. 2008. "Wiseguy: William Shatner." *Details.* Available online: http://men.style.com/details/features/full?id=content_6267. Access date: August 12, 2008.

Kopeikina, L. 2005. *The Right Decision Every Time: How to Reach Perfect Clarity on Tough Decisions.* Upper Saddle River, NJ: Prentice Hall.

Leider, R., and Shapiro, D. 2002. *Repacking Your Bags: Lighten Your Load for the Rest of Your Life.* San Francisco: Berrett-Koehler.

Levoy, G. 1998. *Callings: Finding and Following an Authentic Life.* New York: Three Rivers Press.

Martin, C. A., and Tulgan, B. 2002. *Managing the Generation Mix: From Collision to Collaboration.* Amherst, MA: HDR Press.

van Buskirk, E. 2007. "Herbie Hancock Talks Math, Music and Mastering the Tech Toolbox." Wired.com, October 2, 2007. Available online: www.wired.com/entertainment/music/commentary/listeningpost/2007/10/listeningpost_1001. Access date: August 12, 2008.

Williams, J. 2007. "What's This Thing with Boomers Starting Businesses?" StartupNation, June 22, 2007. Available online: www.startupnation.com/blog/entry.asp?ENTRY_ID=619. Access date: August 12, 2008.

Recommended Reading

Belasco, J., and Sayers, R. 1993. *Flight of the Buffalo: Soaring to Excellence, Learning to Let Employees Lead.* New York: Warner Books.

Bridges, W. 1980. *Transitions: Making Sense of Life's Changes.* New York: Addison-Wesley.

Buckingham, B., and Clifton, M. O. 2001. *Now, Discover Your Strengths.* New York: Free Press.

Carnegie, D. 1990. *How to Win Friends and Influence People.* New York: Pocket Books. (Originally published 1936.)

Henderson, E. 2007. *Career Providence: Navigation Principles for the Black Male Mentee.* Federal Way, WA: Henderworks.

Levit, A. 2004. *They Don't Teach Corporate in College: A Twenty-Something's Guide to the Business World*. Franklin Lakes, NJ: Career Press.

Levit, A. 2008. *How'd You Score That Gig? A Guide to the Coolest Jobs and How to Get Them*. New York: Ballantine Books.

Levit, A. 2008. *Success for Hire: Simple Strategies to Find and Keep Outstanding Employees*. Fairfax, VA: ASTD Press.

Pink, D. 2006. *Free Agent Nation: The Future of Working for Yourself*. Lebanon, IN: Warner Books.

Pink, D. 2006. *A Whole New Mind: Why Right-Brainers Will Rule the Future*. New York: Riverhead Trade.

Richards, D. 1997. *Artful Work: Awakening Joy, Meaning, and Commitment in the Workplace*. New York: Berkley Trade.

Richards, D. 2004. *The Art of Winning Commitment: Ten Ways Leaders Can Engage Minds, Hearts, and Spirits*. New York: AMACOM.

Richards, D. 2005. *Is Your Genius at Work? Four Key Questions to Ask Before Your Next Career Move*. Mountain View, CA: Davies-Black Publishing.

Sanders, T. 2005. *Likeability Factor*. New York: Crown.

Schachter-Shalomi, Z. 1995. *From Age-ing to Sage-ing: A Profound New Vision for Growing Older*. New York: Warner Books.

Zander, R. S., and Zander, B. 2000. *The Art of Possibility: Transforming Personal and Professional Life*. New York: Penguin.

Acknowledgments

Hip & Sage would not have come to fruition had it not been for the contributions of many caring people. Thanks to my husband, Bill, who supports my sometimes-frenetic writing style with hand-crafted gourmet meals and generous supplies of chocolate.[1] Thanks to my editor, Laura Lawson, who both allowed and encouraged me to go outside the traditional business book "box" with *Hip & Sage*. Thanks to Mark Morrow from ASTD Press for encouraging me to take on the project and for bringing Laura and me together.[2] I thank my friend Leigh Strinsky for being a sounding board and my HipandSage.com Web site designer.

Thanks to all the hip and sage folks who listened, commented, and shared their thoughts on what it means to be hip and sage, including Susan Ayers Walker, Effenus Henderson, Robert Levit, Nancy Lewis, and Oliver Picher.[3] Thanks, Alexandra Levit, for sharing your expertise regarding generation-based

1. You can find my husband's Web sites here: www.billhaneberg.com and www.haneberg .com. I have not been able to talk him into starting a blog yet.

2. I have had the pleasure of writing several books for ASTD Press: www.astd.org/content/ publications/ASTDPress.

3. Susan Ayers Walkers is a hip and sage tech writer and the managing director of SmartSilvers: www.astd.org/content/publications/ASTDPress. Effenus Henderson's Web site is here: www.henderworks.com/index.htm. He recently wrote a book called *Career Providence: Navigation Principles for the Black Male Mentee*, which is listed in the References and Recommended Reading section. And Oliver Picher's blog is called Fun with Networking: http://funwithnetworking.com.

relationship-building strategies and for being a longtime supporter of my books and blogs.

I would also like to thank Dick Richards for brainstorming with me on the phone and being a sage mentor on all matters sage. Dick and I have never met but have been pals in the online world for several years. Thanks to Dan Pink for first participating in a great brainstorming conversation and then, second, allowing me to have a little fun with it in the Introduction.

And I would like to thank Ralph Stayer for being the inspiring leader in the brown cowboy boots who got me thinking about sageness back in Dayton, Ohio, in 1997.[4]

---

4. Ralph is CEO of Johnsonville Foods: www.johnsonville.com/home/press-room/corp-info/bios-ralph-c-stayer. His best-selling book is *Flight of the Buffalo: Soaring to Excellence, Learning to Let Employees Lead.* I highly recommend the book to all managers and leaders.

About the Author

Lisa Haneberg is an expert with twenty-five years' experience in management, leadership, and personal and organizational success. She consults on the subjects of organization development, management and leadership training, and human resources and has worked for and with several Fortune 500 companies, including Black & Decker, Intel, Mead Paper, and Amazon.com. Haneberg also offers integrated training solutions and individual and group coaching services. She is an enthusiastic, fun presenter and speaker available to address a variety of leadership and management topics. She has written ten books, as well as numerous articles and essays, and authors a popular blog called Management Craft. She also hosts a podcast called "Fireside Chats About Management and Leadership." Visit her on her Web site: www.lisahaneberg.com.

OTHER BOOKS BY LISA HANEBERG:

High Impact Middle Management: Solutions for Today's Busy Managers (Adams Media, 2005)

Organization Development Basics (ASTD Press, 2005)

Coaching Basics (ASTD Press, 2006)

Focus Like a Laser Beam: 10 Ways to Do What Matters Most (Jossey-Bass, 2006)

Two Weeks to a Breakthrough: How to Zoom Toward Your Goal in 14 Days or Less (Jossey-Bass, 2007)

10 Steps to Be a Successful Manager (ASTD Press, 2007)

Developing Great Managers: 20 Power Hours (ASTD Press, 2008)